PRASE FOR MARY KOLE

"*Writing Interiority* is for all writers ready to level up. Once again, Mary Kole has delivered an entire master class within one volume. I was fortunate enough to work under Mary's tutelage a couple of years ago in the Story Mastermind writing program (aka the best thing I ever did for my craft), and this book is a close second. It digs into the ins and outs of developing your character's inner monologue—something many writers struggle with. Mary touches upon the concept within *Writing Irresistible Kidlit*, and this book picks up where that left off. I highly recommend *Writing Interiority* for your next craft book."

ZANE RÉ-BLOOM

"*Writing Interiority* is crafted for guaranteed learning. Awesome reference tool to assist your writing endeavors. The craft and techniques contained within the lines are a goldmine for those wishing to find joy and new directions in their writing. The book is written to spark maximum reading and retention so writers can unlock their full potential, understand and demystify important concepts. Mary Kole is amazing in writing talent and full mastery ... only someone with understanding can make this look so simple. A very rewarding read, so stick with it, give it time, [and it will] supercharge your writing."

JANIS SMITH

"The craft world needed *Writing Interiority*! Such a difficult concept to do right if it doesn't come naturally. This book will give me better tools to improve my skills. It was broken up so clearly and logically."

WHITNEY

"*Writing Interiority* explains step-by-step how to create and convey character thoughts, feelings, reactions and interpretations, expectations, and inner struggles on the page. With examples from more than fifty books, it is a masterclass on the topic and I'm sure I will reference it for years to come. I've recommended it to all my writing friends as a must-read book on the topic of creating engaging characters that readers are compelled to read about. Thank you Mary for writing such an invaluable resource."

JAMIE WILLIS

"Mary truly is amazing! Thanks to her, I have learned so much about writing. She made me laugh. She made me cry. She made me a better writer!"

M. CHURCHILL

"I've read many books on the craft of writing, and *Writing Irresistible Kidlit* is among the best. I've never been so excited to get to the keyboard."

ALAN HARELL

"The advice is wonderful, thoughtful, and so clearly written that no writer could read *Writing Irresistible Kidlit* and not walk away with something gained from it."

ASHLEE W.

"*Writing Irresistible Kidlit* is hands-down the best writing book I've read in years. It's a masterclass in a book."

ALISON S.

"I can't begin to say how helpful *Writing Irresistible Kidlit* has been for my own writing journey."

JOEL A.

"*Writing Irresistible Picture Books* is insightful, invaluable, and incredibly thorough! It's a must-have for anyone who aspires to write picture books and a great resource for those who are looking to hone their craft. I've already sent the link to writers I know."

ELLE

"After writing a novel, unpublished writers inhabit an unguided middle space between not being important enough to warrant industry attention, and needing professional feedback to see how they stack up in the market. That is where Mary Kole lives. Her advice is sound, she pulls no punches, and if you listen to her, your work will improve."

ANDRES FAZA

"I would highly recommend learning from Mary Kole to anyone seriously looking to improve their writing."

KATE K.

"Mary is a top professional in the industry and her advice is on-point and actionable. Having Mary on your team will no doubt improve your pitch, manuscript, query, or whatever you're writing."

ELANA I.

"Mary Kole brings years of solid experience and insight to the art of writing literature for younger audiences."

ROBIN

"From now on, if I see a writing craft book with Mary Kole's name on it, I will hit the 'one click purchase' button without a second thought. She respects writers. She feels for writers. She understands writers. She knows exactly what insights writers need as they work. *Writing Irresistible Kidlit* is possibly the very best book on writing craft I have read in twenty-five years."

SPROCKET

"Mary Kole made me feel a renewed enthusiasm toward my writing goals."

SUSAN

"*Writing Irresistible Kidlit* is quite simply, the best 'how to' book on novel writing that I've ever read and probably ever will read in my life."

CAROL

"Mary Kole helped me to find my way. Her suggestions on my query letter are just what I needed to begin fearlessly searching for a place to call my own. I now consider Mary Kole my secret weapon."

TRACY

"*Writing Irresistible Kidlit* is the perfect blend of technical 'how to' guidance mixed with a healthy dose of encouragement. If anything I write in the future ever sells, I feel I may owe Ms. Kole a royalty for her shaping input from this book."

A. GABLE

"Mary Kole knows all that a story needs to be to be successful in today's market."

R. TATE

"I'm a big fan of everything Mary Kole does and this book was no exception. I learned so much reading Mary's feedback on the various components of each query letter in *Irresistible Query Letters*."

JAMIE L.

"Kole is clearly passionate about her work and the world of kidlit, and that passion spills over the pages of *Writing Irresistible Kidlit*."

ASHLEY B.

SHOW AND TELL

GOING BEYOND CREATIVE WRITING'S MOST
ENDURING PARADIGM

MARY KOLE

GOOD
STORY
PUBLISHING

"Show and Tell: Going Beyond Creative Writing's Most Enduring Paradigm"
By Mary Kole

1. Reference / Writing, Research, and Publishing Guides / Writing

FIRST EDITION
Ebook ISBN: 978-1-939162-21-2
Print ISBN: 978-1-939162-22-9

Cover Design: Kaylee Pereyra
Editing: Amy Wilson
Author Photo: Joe Ferrucci
Oprah Meme on p. 63 Generated Using: Imgflip.com
Printed in the United States of America

To my editorial clients over the years, who have taught me more than I ever could've imagined.

ABOUT THE AUTHOR

A former literary agent, Mary Kole knows the ins and outs of the publishing industry. She founded Mary Kole Editorial in 2013 to provide consulting and developmental editing services to writers across all categories and genres. She started Good Story Company in 2019 to create valuable content like the Thriving Writers Podcast, Good Story YouTube channel, and the Thriving Writers membership community. Her Story Mastermind small group workshop intensives help writers level up their craft, and she offers done-for-you revision and ghostwriting with Manuscript Studio. She also develops unique and commercial *New York*

Times and *USA Today* best-selling intellectual property for middle grade, young adult, and adult readers with Bittersweet Books, alongside literary agent John Cusick and #1 *New York Times* best-seller Julie Murphy.

Mary has appeared at regional, national, and international writing conferences for the SCBWI, Writer's Digest, Penn Writers, Writer's League of Texas, San Francisco Writers Conference, WIFYR, Writing Day, NINC, and many others. Her guest lectures have taken her to Harvard, the Ringling College of Art and Design, the Highlights Foundation, and more. Mary's recorded video classes can be found online at Writing Mastery Academy, Writing Blueprints, Udemy, and LinkedIn Learning.

Mary holds an MFA in Creative Writing and began her publishing career with a literary agency internship and the Kidlit blog, which she started in 2009. She has worked at Chronicle Books, the Andrea Brown Literary Agency, and Movable Type Management. Her books are *Writing Irresistible Kidlit: The Ultimate Guide to Crafting Fiction for Young Adult and Middle Grade Readers* from Writer's Digest Books / Penguin Random House, and *Irresistible Query Letters, Writing Irresistible Picture Books, How to Write a Book Now, Writing Interiority, Writing Irresistible First Pages, Show and Tell: Going Beyond Creative Writing's Most Enduring Paradigm,* and several companion workbooks, all from Good Story Publishing.

Originally from the San Francisco Bay Area, she lives with her three children, husband, two pugs, and a cat, in Minneapolis, MN.

MARY KOLE

"Receiving Mary's feedback on my novel has been one of the best things that has happened to my writing in recent years. Thanks to her, I see the possibilities in my book and also feel like a fire has been lit under me to continue. I know the work is not yet done, but today—*today*—I feel like it's possible."

ANONYMOUS

facebook.com/goodstoryco

x.com/goodstoryco

instagram.com/goodstorycompany

linkedin.com/company/goodstorycompany

pinterest.com/goodstorycompany

tiktok.com/@goodstoryco

youtube.com/goodstory

bsky.app/profile/goodstory.bsky.social

AI TRANSPARENCY STATEMENT

1. No original text in this book has been *generated* using AI, such as automatic drafting based on an LLM's understanding of existing text.
2. No original text in this book has been *suggested* using AI. This might include asking ChatGPT for an outline.
3. No original text in this book has been *improved* using AI. An example is a system like Grammarly, which offers suggestions to reorder sentences or words to increase a clarity score. The author improved this text the hard way, through human feedback and revision.
4. Original text in this book has been *corrected* using AI (Microsoft Word's standard spelling and grammar check) but suggestions for spelling and grammar have been reviewed, then accepted or rejected, based on the author's human discretion.

Special Circumstances:

This book features excerpts from 53 novels. Excerpts are clearly identified and the author cannot make the above warranties for any text that is not original to this guide.

This AI Transparency Statement text is adapted from one Kester Brewin developed and published in *The Guardian*.[i]

TABLE OF CONTENTS

CONTENT WARNING

This writing guide features excerpts from 53 published works and summarizes contextually relevant elements of their plots. What this means for you: There will be spoilers for certain books. I will generally mention the book's title before discussing it, so if you don't want anything spoiled, skip that section.

More consequentially, these stories deal with a number of potentially difficult topics, as novels and memoirs often reflect and even amplify the most dramatic events life has to offer. These topics include historical human slavery, colonialism, drug and alcohol abuse, murder, infertility, abortion, child loss, mental health crisis, stalking, domestic assault, and suicidal ideation. Go easy on yourself as you read if you find any of these subjects triggering, and make sure you have support. This is a writing guide, and I would hate for the subject matter in certain excerpts to overshadow their intended educational purpose.

There's also the occasional swear word (theirs and mine … mostly mine). Sorry, Mom!

INTRODUCTION

At some point in your creative writing life, a well-meaning English teacher, storytelling guide, literary agent, or even acquisitions editor told you to "show, don't tell." I know this because I've been working in publishing and teaching the craft since 2009—first as a literary agent, now as a freelance editor and IP developer—and I have given this *exact* note seventy trillion times.

If nobody's ever told you this, I'm so glad to slide into your creative journey DMs first. But I don't think I've met a single writer who hasn't already heard this advice, even if they're not always adhering to it. Even if they hate it. And if you *do* hate it, good. Because I'm frustrated with it, too. Whatever your situation, if you're reading this book, that means you're ready to dismantle and reframe this old chestnut to work for *you*.

Don't fret. Your English teacher isn't going to come to your house and throttle you with a copy of the *Chicago Manual of Style*. (A cutting remark jotted in red pen is more an English teacher's weapon of choice, anyway.) I promise.

What I'm asking for in this guide is an open mind and a bit of trust. We're heading into uncharted waters—those which churn beyond Writing 101.

Don't get me wrong. There is actually wisdom to the "show, don't tell" maxim (I'll cover that in the following chapter). It serves a valuable purpose in anyone's creative development.

But I *also* maintain to this day—in fact, more strongly than ever—that it has single-handedly wrought more ineffective and self-conscious prose than any other idea. "Show, don't tell" is not just a sentence-level piece of advice. It tends to affect a writer's entire approach. And it leaves a lot to be desired.

It's time we take a long, hard, and critical look at something we've all been following blindly. Because today's most effective and marketable narrative writing thrives on nuance. The space *between* "show" and "tell." That's what we're going to explore.

The Publishing Market

The current traditional publishing landscape is more competitive than ever before. And you're not immune to its pressures if you choose to self-publish because you're still competing for the same audience's eyeballs and dollars. Your future readers' tastes have also largely been shaped and led by traditional publishing. They'll borrow your work on Kindle Unlimited or read the sample and make their decisions. If they find you haven't mastered contemporary storytelling techniques, they'll move on.

Today's readers are savvier than ever about narrative craft, whether they're consciously aware of it or not. As pressure rises, you'll want to learn and grow as much as possible in your own voice and style. The industry is largely outside of your control. What you know and how you wield it, however, are yours and yours alone. No matter what happens with an individual project, market trends, or the outside world.

Modern fiction and memoir require sophistication because the bar keeps rising higher every year. Readers want to inhabit a richly imagined character with deep POV and close narrative distance. They also want to get swept up in a finely tuned plot. Remember, today's audiences are now used to stepping into the perspectives of countless personalities, influencers, and real humans on social media. Sometimes thousands of times per day. They're privy to thoughts, feelings, and inner struggles delivered into the front-facing camera of countless cell phones on an infinite scroll.

This mode of perceiving information about a character[1] has taught your readership—whose leisure time you're asking for when you offer them a story—to sink into the intimate layers of the people they're intrigued by. This is why I spent so much time developing my previous writing guide, *Writing Interiority: Crafting Irresistible Characters*. Getting below the surface of POV protagonists is crucial to fostering audience connection.

And this is exactly where we run into issues with "show, don't tell." It encourages you to play at the superficial levels of appearance, physicality, and action. These are important storytelling ingredients, but they're merely a starting point. They're also woefully unequipped to help writers reach the marrow inside their POV characters, which is what we should all be doing in order to captivate readers and generate a fan base.

Without further ado, let's unpack the paradoxical wisdom *and*

---

1. Make no mistake, the people on social media are portraying a character, even if they claim vulnerability and authenticity as their personal brands.

limitations of "show, don't tell," and what you can do instead to elevate your storytelling.

THE WISDOM AND PITFALLS OF "SHOW, DON'T TELL"

If you're like most writers, you already know that "telling" simply means stating a character's emotion, objective, motivation, backstory, or other key attributes in the text itself. Think, "She was angry," and, "He is a nice guy, the kind who'd give a buddy the shirt off his back."

Meanwhile, "showing" is the practice of describing some of these same ideas, emotions, and character traits through action. Think, "She balled her fists up into tight knots," and the narrative description of the character giving someone the shirt off his literal back. As such, many well-meaning creative writers make the following delineation: scenes are for showing, summaries are for telling, and that's that. Consider these more balanced definitions instead:

Telling: Explicit statements of story and character realities, where the author or narrator speaks directly to the reader in an expository or explanatory manner. This gets in the way of reader extrapolation and discovery by overtly explaining thematic, character, and plot elements. You should absolutely avoid passive telling, but some telling is appropriate and warranted, as long as it occurs in concert with showing and leaves room for audiences to participate.

Showing: An action-based method of displaying a character's inner life via external means, from dialogue to movement to the sensation in their physical body. This allows readers to play along by interpreting what's happening below the surface, extrapolating why, and inferring the deeper meanings and ramifications. It also reminds writers to keep their stories active with narrative and scene. But if you're only showing throughout, this approach can present some unique challenges and get in the way of character and story context and specificity.

Here are some very derivative examples of showing and telling, side by side, which are intended to make an obvious point. The telling instances will be aligned to the left, while showing is on the right:

He was angry.

>He huffed and slammed the door.

She was nervous.

>Her stomach fluttered with butterflies.

She fell head over heels in love.

>Her heart hammered in her chest.

He was nice.

He pulled the cat out of the storm drain.

Pretty straightforward, right? "Show, don't tell" does a brilliant job of reminding us that storytelling is more than just explaining a story. After all, the art and craft of narrative involves so many *other* elements. A "story" like, "Once upon a time, a knight battled a dragon and struggled to overcome his obstacles" does absolutely nothing for an audience. It is the most basic framework for a narrative, but nobody would mistake it for a compelling yarn. Readers want deeper insight into character, narration, action, adventure, emotion, dialogue, description … and every other craft component element involved in spinning a tale. If we simply state everything outright, we're writing a caption, bumper sticker, or brochure, not a story. "Show, don't tell" reinforces these ideas to keep aspiring writers away from simplistic copy that gives readers nothing to do.

But this is also where "show, don't tell" hits a barrier pretty quickly. Unfortunately, in many manuscripts, "show, don't tell" translates to a lot of physical descriptions, gestures, and clichés. A visual rendering of events with absolutely no connection to a character's inner life. This is a dead-end approach, too.

Pure "telling" can be bad (though I'm going to introduce you to many exceptions in this guide). However, pure "showing" is also ineffective. These represent the extremes of storytelling, and you're never going to find the marrow of nuance there.

And the reason we're aiming for nuance has everything to do with audience engagement and how readers read.

How Readers Read

Readers are detectives who like to be actively involved in uncovering and interpreting information. If you simply tell them everything you want them to know, you risk them feeling like outsiders with no stake in the story. "She was angry" might be true and clear, but it doesn't ask anything of the audience. It's disposable information and doesn't elicit empathy. Reading the word "angry" won't make me angry myself. I won't be thinking about why the character is feeling this way, and I certainly won't empathize.

"Show, don't tell" would have you do something like:

> She slammed her fist on the table.

This is the bare minimum. But both "She was angry" *and* the above are flat. We get absolutely no sense of character or context. Let's try this instead:

> If that no-good, rotten jerk ever darkened her doorstep again, she'd knock him into next Thursday.

The latter example communicates anger in a colorful and engaging way, using interiority and voice. It lets the reader draw the connection between the prose and the emotion of "angry." Leaving an opening for interpretation invites the audience to reach out, emote, and relate to a character's feelings. As a result, readers take personal ownership of the story, which is key.

Bad telling, at its core, is incredibly condescending. It doesn't trust the reader to do their job of discovering the story and peeling back its emotional layers. In the case of most people who actively choose to be readers, it's a job they love. Egregious telling in a manuscript feels like a pat on the head.

It also (perhaps unintentionally) communicates a lack of writing confidence. It's as if the writer doesn't think they've done a good job of making the story speak for itself. You shouldn't approach your reader relationship from this place of insecurity. I know, I know, this is *a lot* easier said than done.

But once you realize you don't have to explain (or when you *do* explain, you're doing it purposefully), you can trust yourself to tell the story *and* trust your reader to follow. It's a terrifying and liberating breakthrough, and something I hope you experience as you start applying the concepts in this guide to your own work.

The rudimentary "show, don't tell" dichotomy doesn't give writers or readers the full story. If you unlearn what you think you know about this advice, you might start noticing telling all over published books. Has there been some kind of massive error? Does publishing have a huge double standard, enabling a shady cabal of writers who are "allowed" to tell? No. Because there are multiple types of telling, and not all are bad. In fact, some are downright necessary.

Good and Bad Telling

This is where I draw a distinction between what I call "bad telling" and "good telling." First, let's discuss "bad telling" and the writing elements you should largely avoid stating outright until you're more comfortable with your own personal style of telling:[1]

- **Inherent Personality Traits**: Don't outright explain personality traits central to your character's core

---

1. Though, again, you'll see published exceptions throughout this guide, and we'll talk about what they're doing and why they work each time.

identity, whether the protagonist is a "good sport" or a "loose cannon."

- **Emotions**: When readers hear that someone is "hurt" or "sad" or even "happy," this is the most superficial expression of an emotion. The "why" behind a feeling is almost always more interesting than the feeling itself. This should either be provided in context within the scene or communicated using interiority. There's also the thought that triggers the feeling, and its aftermath. None of these juicy ideas can be explored if you're merely labeling the emotion.

Take, for example, this straightforward "bad telling":

> After everything it took to get to this moment, he was excited to see what happened. But there was also a shiver of fear beneath the surface. What if he wasn't chosen?

The above delivers information but there's no sense of voice or emotional inflection. You'll notice we name emotions outright with "excited" and "fear," but they don't really do much justice to the swirl of competing emotions the character might be feeling. The information lies flat on the page.

Contrast it with this:

> This was it, and he couldn't have been more ready. Six months of training, three trials, and now he balanced on the precipice. This could either set him up for the rest of his life or, well, end it. The dragon gate opened.

Not only are the ideas of "excited" and "fear" communicated with more nuance—as the reader must work to unearth them from the prose—but we get information about the length of the character's preparation for this scene (and even a sense of what it looks like—a literal and figurative precipice in front of the dragon gate). Thanks to interiority, the data is seamlessly inserted without calling much overt attention to itself. And yes, before you ask, interiority is almost always delivered through telling.

The second example above involves "good telling," which you may not have felt comfortable exploring before. I'm here to tell you that it can be perfectly appropriate to make factual statements in creative writing, as long as these are balanced with action. Certain categories of information can and *should* be conveyed with interiority and narration.

Sometimes, there's really no good way to say it … except to say it.

The below story elements fit under the "good telling" umbrella:

- **Self-Perception**: How does the protagonist see themselves? Is this in conflict with anything or anyone else? Does their self-perception change as they go through the story? Do they shift from their objective to their need, and what are the ramifications of this transition? (We'll discuss this in Chapter 4.)
- **Objective and Motivation**: What does the character want, and why do they want it? (See Chapter 4 as well.)
- **Backstory**: What are some significant past events which have shaped a character, for better or worse (or both)? (Check out Chapter 5 for more.)
- **Worldview**: A character's values, belief system, and worldview are impacted by both nature and nurture (aka backstory). They play a key role in your character's objectives, needs, decisions, and sense of self. (We'll explore this in Chapter 5 as well.)

- **Wound and Need**: What's the protagonist's underlying need and wound (the genesis of their need)? (This relates to backstory gets a deep dive in Chapter 6.)
- **Inner Struggle**: What's the biggest thing they're grappling with, on a personal level (in general) or in difficult times (in particular)? (More on this in Chapter 6 as well.)
- **Plot Tension and Conflict**: What are the story's sources of external, plot-based conflict? What's happening to the character in their overall development arc or place in the narrative? (See Chapter 8.)
- **Stakes**: What are the consequences of a specific event or choice? What might happen if the character is successful or unsuccessful in a present or future action? And, most importantly, why does it matter to them—and to readers? (We'll explore this in Chapter 8 as well.)
- **Historical World-Building and Magic System Context**: If you're writing in a speculative, fantasy, science fiction, or historical genre, you'll want to include details about the world or era, why it works the way it does, and how these issues affect character development and plot. But world-building also plays a key role in contemporary realistic stories, just in subtler ways. (See Chapter 10.)

Certain information is difficult to transmit to readers without it being explicitly stated somewhere. So now that we have a more complex overview of telling, let's really explore some common shortcomings of showing.

Bad Showing

Funnily enough, the writers who are showing too much—doing the "right" type of writing!—are sometimes struggling the most in the interiority and nuance departments. Their characters display the same cluster of physical clichés for emotion—hammering hearts, stomach butterflies, white-knuckle fingers on steering wheels—over and over, but offer no deeper insights for readers to explore. A major benefit of strong interiority and good telling is its ability to provide seamless context. Writers often struggle with establishing information and backstory. It can be tough to draw the line between good and bad telling.

Just so we're clear, here are the limitations of pure showing:

- **It can be painfully obvious**. Take, for example:
  - "Her lower lip protruded in a pout."
    - The pout isn't adding nuance. It's adding redundancy, especially if readers also have the context of this scene and know why she's upset. If the body language matches the dialogue or action perfectly, then it's not deepening the scene. It's just underlining it in highlighter.
- **It doesn't actually reveal interior life**.
  - "Going very still" and trembling are basic physical beats that might be done by *any* generic character in a moment of heightened tension. Body language is all surface, no psychology. It's puppetry, not point of view.
- **It tries to perform emotion instead of evoking it**.
  - You know when an actor does "crying" by scrunching their face and blinking a lot, and it just feels fake? This is that, but on the page. Familiar physical gestures feel pre-programmed. Real

9

emotion in fiction and memoir works when it
surprises us or complicates the moment.
- **It's weirdly infantilizing**.
  - A protagonist simply miming or gesticulating
    undercuts the power of the scene and makes the
    character seem emotionally stunted instead of
    something more interesting.
- **It's generic**.
  - Nothing surprises readers when it comes to well-
    worn physical clichés. That's not storytelling.
    That's just place-holding until you figure out how
    your characters actually tick.

This kind of showing is flat because it's generic, redundant,
emotionally shallow, and simplistic. It's "showing" that
doesn't actually show anything meaningful. Once you start to
do the real work of showing *and* telling, you can offer:

- A surprising physical reaction;
- An emotionally contradictory beat;
- A gesture that reveals history or desire or shame; or
- An explanation, but with voice and specificity.

Many writers know when a character needs extra dimension
but are often unsure how to provide it without hitting readers
over the head. Interiority is an elegant way to deploy not only
emotion but information. You can also use it to offer reasons
why both matter. When you support your showing with *some*
telling, the result is an alchemy that's greater than the sum of
your craft parts.

The point is simple. I don't really care *that* a character is
crying. Tears shown on someone's face aren't going to make
me commiserate. I also especially don't care that a character is
merely thinking. This is a big one. "Thoughts whirled around

in her head." Okay. That's nice. Anything more specific? And? So?

Specificity is key. Characters are individuals. Everyone experiences emotions and events differently. If you're only showing the external, a whole layer is missing. Why is the character crying? What's the thought that touched off the tears?

We all know what it's like to be overcome with emotion, but it's often a very specific thought or image sparking the waterworks. The physical body can only tell us so much. Then we have to dig deeper.

In fact, for our first excerpt from the shelves, I'll present the moment of a cry catalyst from *Vera Wong's Unsolicited Advice for Murderers* by Jesse Q. Sutanto. Notice how the situation is serious, but the interiority is actually quite ... cheeky:

> But last night, after ten married years and fourteen altogether as a couple, Marshall told her unceremoniously that he'd "made it" and was finally leaving her "sorry ass." *Honestly*, Julia thinks as she helps Emma push a particularly stubborn piece of Lego into place, *there is nothing sorry about my ass*. She keeps her ass in very good shape, damn it. And it's this ridiculous thought that smacks into her with sudden ruthlessness and triggers hot tears rushing into her eyes. Who the hell cares about her ass right now? *Although*, a small voice pipes up as she stifles her sobs, *it really is a very good one.*[i]

Not exactly what you might've expected Julia thinking about after the disillusion of her marriage, no?

Interiority and good telling transcend the limitations of showing, which is why they're such crucial tools to add to your ever-expanding understanding of writing and storytelling.

But What About Voice?

Guess what? Voice is telling. Voice isn't description. Voice isn't dialogue. Voice isn't mood.

Voice is the lens. The filter. It's how a story tells itself. Which means: it is 100% telling. So when someone tries to apply "Show, don't tell" to writing style or voice, it's a fool's errand. Voice doesn't show anything. It *is* the telling—the what and especially the *how*. Voice is the character telling the story in real time.

Consider this:

> He didn't cry. That would give them something to talk about.

You're not showing us what happened. You're telling us how this narrator interprets the action. Their fear. Their bitterness. Their social context. Their survival instinct. Their humor. That's not an objective description of events—it's a subjective, emotional, stylized spin on the world. That's voice.

After all, can anyone accuse the above *Vera Wong's Unsolicited Advice for Murderers* excerpt of not having voice?

Writers often confuse "neutral prose" with "showing." Somewhere along the way, we got this idea that "showing" means stripping the prose of personality: using short, invisible sentences; avoiding filter words; pretending there's no narrator at all. That's not showing. That's just bleaching the voice out of the story.

"Showing" is demonstrating character and story through action. But voice is interpretation and implication. It's how a protagonist's personality bleeds into narration. So trying to remove telling from voice is like trying to remove yeast from bread. You *can* do it, but what you get is flat, dry, and deeply unsatisfying.

Gatekeepers will often say "I'll know it when I see it" when it comes to voice and style because both are a felt experience. Agents and editors say they want voice—but they can't define it. They say things like:

- "I just want something that grabs me."
- "The voice needs to feel authentic."
- "I need to hear the narrator in my head."

And those are all true.

But what they don't say is: Voice *is* telling. It's not subtle or objective. It's a layer, a filter, a lens. And, most importantly, it's a decision writers must commit to.

So let's destroy this false binary. "Show, don't tell" makes writers think that telling is always passive, flat, or weak—and that voice has to emerge through action or dialogue only. No. Show through behavior. Tell with voice. Do both with intent.

One of my favorite writing quotes is:

"The first draft is just you telling yourself the story."

TERRY PRATCHETT

And sometimes readers need to be told, too. The key is figuring out your personal recipe of when, how, where, and why you choose to tell. Then leaving the old "show, don't tell" maxim in the dust.

2

UNDERSTANDING TELLING

Not all telling is bad, but lazy telling is. Good telling can accelerate pacing—or the perceived speed at which narrative moves, bridge scenes and time, deliver interiority and characterizing details with clarity, and anchor voice and tone. The types of telling that work especially well offer summary narration (or "compressed narration"), interiority ("She hated herself for saying it, but here she went anyway"), thematic commentary ("Love was madness"), and precise emotional labeling ("It was rage that *burned*"), but only if it's earned within the context of the story.

One of the topics I explored quite heavily in *Writing Interiority* was narrative distance, or how close or far from the action the POV narrator is. With something like first-person present tense, we are right there in the action. The character has no choice but to narrate what they perceive because they *are* the lens. With an omniscient narrator in past tense, we can be far, or we can be granted access to a character's interiority, which brings us closer. Still, in the most distant examples, the lens floats above the scene, watching from on high, and we miss out on that essential—not to mention contemporary and desirable—connection to any one POV character.

When we're applying showing and telling to the spectrum of narrative distance, it might be helpful to think of telling as distant (or potentially distant) and showing as close. With showing, we're right there in the action—physical, sensorial, visceral, and unfolding in real-time present narration. Telling introduces some distance—filtered, temporal, contemplative, analyzed, or summarized. While this seems like an obvious argument in support of "show, don't tell," know that you can intentionally wield telling to add this layer of distance and reflection.

This guide is all about finding the nuances between two major storytelling and craft concepts that are carelessly shoved down writers' throats by well-meaning teachers. So there's going to be a certain amount of "yes/and" and "both things can be true" embedded in our conversation.

Too much showing, as we've established, can push into your reader's face and breathe down their neck at all times. And just as you want to balance action and information in storytelling, sometimes you need to take a step back. Intentional telling allows you to create irony, show a character dissociating, transition between scenes with minimal logistical data, and add a crucial veneer of lived experience that makes your storytelling irresistible to readers.

When to Show, When to Tell

Though it's impossible to offer exact guidelines for every story, genre, [1] and target audience, I do have some broad-strokes advice for when both showing and telling are most appropriate to add to your storytelling strategy mix.

Showing is the best approach when:

---

1. Though I'll dig into this topic more in Chapter 11.

- stakes are high;
- a character is making a decision or having a change of heart in the moment, and it can be shown in action; and
- conflict or relationship developments are unfolding in the present narrative.

On the flip side, telling can be used:

- in the transitions between scenes;
- to summarize irrelevant action which would otherwise bog your narrative down with logistics; and
- to provide emotional context or character commentary for events that are unfolding, those that have already happened, or ones a character might anticipate.

Show for emotional escalation and plot movement. Tell for compression, clarity, and control. However, you have to also wield telling with authority, confidence, and intention. Something I see a lot in my editorial practice is this odd disconnect between what a writer is telling me and what I perceive as a reader.

Sometimes, this is on purpose—an unreliable narrator can create great engagement if they insist on one thing, but a reader's own impressions are throwing up red flags. In this case, audiences who are drawn to this type of protagonist will yearn to discover what the reality is.

Unreliable Narrators: When I first started agenting, *Liar* by Justine Larbalestier was setting the young adult (YA) world on fire as *the* example of an unreliable narrator. This craft term refers to a narrator who is willfully shaping a reader's perception of them in a manipulative (and often self-aggrandizing) direction. This is done with telling and assertions meant to lead or mislead; by selectively showcasing only those actions and events that give readers a certain perception; by withholding crucial data (often reserved for a climactic reveal); or a combination of all of the above. It's important to know that unreliable narrators must be unreliable for a reason. Whether it's to pull off a huge twist (*We Were Liars* by E. Lockhart); to seed second-guessing and doubt about a character's state of mind in a story with a psychological element (*Clever Little Thing* by Helena Echlin); to reserve a deep, foundational wound until readers really relate to the character (*Eleanor Oliphant Is Completely Fine* by Gail Honeyman); or to pull off a story-length experiment in perception (*The Guest* by Emma Cline, which I excerpt in Chapter 5). Unreliable narrators are fun to play around with and frequently appear in mystery, thriller, and suspense stories, among others. This said, if a character plays with them for no reason, readers might feel jerked around. Does the story work without the narrator being unreliable? Are there other facets to the character? As with any other kind of protagonist, an unreliable narrator must be part of a cohesive whole.

Oftentimes, though, the disconnect between what readers are told or shown, and what they themselves experience, is unintentional. This can be extremely disengaging. For example, a narrator (or character) can insist the following about her romantic interest:

He's the most moral man a gal could think to
meet.[2]

But then readers see the man in action and he's not a values-
led creature at all. He's lying to the main character, going
behind her back, and making a very different impression on
readers than he is on the POV protagonist or narrator.

Well, now what? Readers will invariably trust what they
perceive and the impressions they're gathering about your
story. Even if the protagonist or narrator is reasonable and
reliable most of the time, if they start *telling* one thing while
the story *shows* another, the audience will always believe their
own experiences. The POV protagonist is usually designed to
be a proxy for your target audience, so any friction feels
uncomfortable.

If this divergence isn't being executed on purpose, watch out.
In the above example, readers will wonder if the protagonist
is so blinded by love that she's missing obvious red flags.
And if those flags are *too* obvious, readers might grow weary
of her swooning and wonder when she's going to realize the
truth. If this gap persists for too long—when readers feel they
know something and are simply waiting for the protagonist
to drop the denial and catch up—you've got issues. We want
protagonists who are sharp and capable of critical thinking,
for the most part. Those are the most compelling perspectives
to inhabit. Delay the light-bulb moment for too long, and
audiences might lose interest.

But a more insidious outcome is possible, too. Readers might
start to doubt you—the writer—if this disconnect persists.
They might wonder whether you really believe what you're
saying, or even whether you're actually capable of rendering

---

2. I don't know why this came out in a Southern accent in my head, nor why
it's got a gee-whiz 1950s flavor, but we're going to roll with it.

a relatable character. You might lose credibility as a storyteller. If you send the signal, even unintentionally, that you're not in control of your craft, readers might worry they're wasting their time.

But there's only so much I can *tell* you in general terms or *show* you with made-up examples. Let's demonstrate these concepts in practice with our first batch of excerpts from the shelves. Some of them include flagrant telling—even "bad telling." I chose them as a shock to the system and to get you thinking differently right away.

From the Shelves

Here's an example of obvious telling about character from the literary novel *Hello Beautiful* by Ann Napolitano:

> On the inside, William knew, he was as uninteresting and muted as his looks. He never spoke at school, and no one played with him. But the boys on the basketball court offered William a chance to be part of something for the first time, without having to talk.[i]

This might seem egregious, the exact kind of bad character telling we called out in Chapter 1. However, notice that William is technically relaying this about himself in close third-person POV, so we start to see his self-perception, a characterizing idea we'll explore more in the following chapter. The above excerpt also comes from page 5 of the story. This is an intergenerational family saga, and the author has tasked herself with the ambitious goal of getting all the siblings on the page quickly. If we don't need to dwell on William's youth—if we just need to fast-forward him to his passion for basketball—this is maybe everything readers require to *get it*.

In another quote from the same story, we meet Julia:

> Julia loved living in this moment, with her life directly in front of her instead of off in the distance. She'd spent her entire childhood waiting to grow up so she could be *here*, ringing all the bells of adulthood.[ii]

With this snippet, we're past the condensed backstory of her major biographical details and in the present moment of the story. The author uses compressed narration, telling, and summary to get us all the way to the cusp of Julia's coming of age. Maybe the finer details of her childhood don't matter. All readers need to know is that she's yearned to be grown all her life. That one detail says a lot about her character, so that's what the author offers. In telling.

Here's another early-on character self-assessment, this time from Opal, the protagonist of the YA speculative novel, *Starling House* by Alix E. Harrow:

> You're never going to be very popular when you wear clothes from the First Christian donation box and shoplift your school supplies, no matter how slick your smile is; the other kids sensed the hunger behind the smile and avoided me out of an animal certainty that, if we were all shipwrecked together, I'd be found six weeks later picking my teeth with their bones.[iii]

This is a great example of voice-infused telling. By offering this self-portrait, Opal communicates class, self-awareness, and story tone all at once. This is telling not as shortcut, but as character definition. We also get a shiver of something macabre—"I'd be found six weeks later picking my teeth with their bones"—to suggest the overall genre and vibe of this project. This hypothetical suggestion goes a long way toward installing an early impression of this protagonist, how she thinks, and how she expresses herself.

We can make it even more direct, as our next protagonist, Alice, explains herself in an email to another character. This is from Sally Rooney's *Beautiful World, Where Are You*, and the publisher went all out, making exclusive bucket hat merch and influencer mailings in support of this release.[3] The below is proof that some telling isn't going to get you automatically dinged. It could even get you lofted into the literary stratosphere:

> I keep encountering this person, who is myself, and I hate her with all my energy. I hate her ways of expressing herself, I hate her appearance, and I hate her opinions about everything. And yet when other people read about her, they believe that she is me. Confronting this fact makes me feel I am already dead.[iv]

This introspective first-person voice uses pure telling to convey internal collapse. The intimacy is suffocating—and effective. Readers aren't being *shown* self-hatred—we're being confessed to in real time. The author has used the email as a frame to get away with explicit telling.

In our next excerpt, from the thriller *The House Across the Lake* by Riley Sager, we get some later-story character analysis from Casey, an actress in a career slump. She is considering what she has become after starting to spy on Tom, her neighbor across the lake, who she's convinced is doing something nefarious:

---

3. I only mention this because those hats have become a bit of a publishing internet meme. IYKYK.

It's also none of my business, a fact I never seriously considered until this moment. Now that I have, I find myself caught between vindication and shame. Tom was wrong to imply I was being obsessive and hysterical. I was worse: a nosy neighbor. A part I've never played before, either onstage or onscreen. In real life, it's not a good fit. In fact, it's downright hypocritical. I, of all people, know what it feels like to have private problems dragged out for public scrutiny. Just because it had been done to me doesn't mean it's okay for me to do it to Tom Royce.[v]

Notice that we can have character self-assessment early in the story (the previous examples all appear within the first dozen pages), or later, as the protagonist develops along their arc. This sample features emotional reflection being used to shift self-perception (and reader perception, too). Casey reevaluates a role she's slipped into, drawing on her own self-judgment to sharpen the stakes. We also get references to what readers already know of her backstory ("I, of all people, know what it feels like to have private problems dragged out for public scrutiny"). But when Casey touches upon this, she can reference her hypocrisy in a voice-driven way, so readers are invited to empathize with her regardless of her flexible value system. Not only do we know what she's talking about, but we know she's aware enough to examine herself in this cold light, to find herself wanting. This kind of real (or feigned) vulnerability can trigger reader connection, even when a protagonist is going off the rails.

The above examples communicate character essence. Let's see some telling about the entire scope of a relationship from a different thriller, *Everyone Who Can Forgive Me Is Dead* by Jenny Hollander:

But I didn't ask, and he didn't say anything else

about it, any of it, and we spent our time together watching TV in silence, like an old married couple who should have divorced years ago. [vi]

This excerpt also orients readers in the protagonist, Charlie's, backstory. The reflective tone offers a brief rise and fall as a stand-in for an entire relationship, and maybe this is what we really need to know about Jordan, the boyfriend in question. Why stretch it out? (Of course, Jordan is a bigger part of this story, but their dating stint is not the primary focus.) This is telling used for emotional compression—summarizing an entire relational dynamic in one voice-driven sentence. The image of an old married couple is apt, comparing this relationship to an archetype readers are familiar with. It's precise, visual, and emotionally weighty without requiring a full scene to spell out the cracks between these two characters.

If we shift over to first-person narration, we can track the evolution of a protagonist's feelings about a secondary character, her father, through telling and interiority. Here's an example from *Happiness Falls* by Angie Kim, a literary novel about a family that breaks apart along ideological lines regarding their son, who has developmental disabilities. Dad has decided to quit his job and stay home with him (and will secretly try some experimental therapies, which will be part of the conflict). The sibling, Mia, is observing (and judging) the moment Dad announces his new plan:

Looking at Dad through this lens, at his grand gesture and grand speech announcing his grand sacrifice—a sliver of what Mom had done for sixteen years without once labeling it a "sacrifice"—it made me hate him. For just a microsecond.

There are moments when something we've idealized all our lives changes and becomes something less. Not by a noticeable amount, just an infinitesimal disappointment. But it's like going from 100 percent to 99.99 percent—imperceptible quantitatively, but dramatically different qualitatively, from flawless to flawed. After this point, I found myself questioning Dad's motives, doubting his perspectives, in a way I hadn't before.[vii]

This scene takes place later in the story, on page 115, like the shift in self-perception we saw from *The House Across the Lake*, above. Mia compresses a shift in emotional perception and worldview into a few lines and this distance allows for judgment after the fact. The voice then shifts to a classic omniscient reflection of the character's worldview. It's universal in tone but personal in purpose. This distance creates space for resonance and theme without abandoning character insight. We also get her unique voice. From the way she talks about her emotions, readers might infer that she's a STEM brain and literal thinker.

Up next is an example of a metaphor or image used to express the quality of life inside a home where the family is grieving the protagonist's older brother, who was killed in a car accident. This comes from the YA novel *Rez Ball* by Byron Graves:

> Those nights rip the stitches off my heart. And the next morning, it feels like we each have to start healing all over again.[viii]

This is emotional telling with imagery, fully earned by the build-up of shown moments before it. This compresses a family's grief cycle into a resonant, memorable metaphor. It also leads the protagonist, Tre, to decide that he *must* pursue basketball in order to make something of himself, since his brother no longer can:

CHAPTER 2

I have to make it.[ix]

How many words would it take to show this instead? Here's an imagined rewrite:

> I stood tall and proud, glancing at my brother's urn on the mantle. Then I saluted him.

But would that have the same power as a simple first-person declaration? Would we know the intention behind the salute? Or would it scan as a generic moment of grief and reverence —an emotional instance, sure, but without the deeper understanding that this protagonist is taking a stand *and* making a commitment, which will translate into his objective.

Once a character is up and running, we must put them into context. One of the most impactful applications of telling is the fleshing out of your story world, including beliefs and cultural values. Here's an example from the literary novel *A Little Life* by Hanya Yanagihara:

> But these were days of self-fulfillment, where settling for something that was not quite your first choice of a life seemed weak-willed and ignoble. Somewhere, surrendering to what seemed to be your fate had changed from being dignified to being a sign of your own cowardice. There were times when the pressure to achieve happiness felt almost oppressive, as if happiness were something that everyone should and could attain, and that any sort of compromise in its pursuit was somehow your fault.[x]

This story is all about the internal and external pressure a group of young people faces to live or be a certain way. The excerpt summarizes the forces at play. Notice we're also using second-person direct address (the "you") to almost *force* relatability. How much of this could've been left to readers to interpret? This story clocks it at an impressive (or excessive, depending on your preferences) 814 pages, so the author decided to really take her time and spell things out. And yet it was shortlisted for a National Book Award and the Man Booker Prize!

Let's pivot to a more dangerous, edgy portrayal of a story's cultural setting, which comes from the speculative novel, *Dead in Long Beach, California* by Venita Blackburn:

> With the concept of Later came the perversion of More. Early humankind clearly had a keen sense of More. They always wanted More: more food, more water, more sex, more reasons to war for food, water, and sex. It wasn't complicated, but once Later entered their consciousness, the limits of More widened to hazardous extremes.[xi]

This narrative labels the forces of human desire as More and Later. We've always had More, but Later (a modern concept) allows it to expand. Whether you agree or not, you can't accuse this excerpt of not having a clear perspective and worldview. It's a stylized, abstract, and philosophical aside that contextualizes the novel's thematic stakes early on. This kind of telling clearly builds the novel's intellectual and emotional scaffolding, which will only be explored by the character development and plotting throughout.

And here's a more straightforward example of backstory about a dystopian world from the YA novel, *Wilder Girls* by Rory Power:

> Emmy was in sixth grade when the Tox happened, and one by one the other girls in her year have crashed headlong into puberty, their first flare-

ups screaming and bursting like fireworks. Now it's finally her turn.

> We listen as she whimpers, her body trembling and seizing. I wonder what she'll get, if it's anything at all. Gills like Mona's, blisters like Cat's, maybe bones like Byatt's or a hand like Reese's, but sometimes the Tox doesn't give you anything—just takes and takes. Leaves you drained and withering.[xii]

This tight first-person POV balances summary telling (the history of "the Tox") with a zoomed-in emotional beat—the narrator's anticipation about Emmy's impending transformation. It's intimate but controlled, using narration to speed through exposition while keeping emotional stakes high. Readers are also intrigued by a curiosity hook that's planted from the beginning—which version of the Tox can Emmy expect, and how will it affect the group and protagonist?

Isn't telling absolutely *everywhere*, now that you start to look at published pieces through this lens?

The trick isn't to avoid telling or to bend yourself into pretzels to try and show *everything*. The trick is to figure out your own personal guidelines of when you'll show, when you'll tell, and how you'll navigate this mix with each individual project.

I've been teaching writing for over fifteen years, and I have personally shared *a lot* of so-called rules. Now I'm peeling back the curtain, because the only rules in writing are those you make for yourself. If you enjoyed these excerpts, hold on to your hat, because you're about to get a whole lot more of them, especially as we discuss the beautiful balancing act of telling as it pertains to character.

3

SHOWING AND TELLING CHARACTER

Bringing a character to life on the printed (or digital) page is one of the biggest challenges any aspiring storyteller faces. Unfortunately—and at the crux of the "show, don't tell" dilemma—you shouldn't just explain[1] who someone is and expect to hook readers. We did see some flagrant telling about character in the previous chapter's examples, but you must understand the utility of those instances. The summaries were reserved for character elements that didn't matter as much. It was backstory the authors decided to speed through in order to get somewhere more interesting.

As we'll see throughout this guide, you must be selective in where you choose to lavish your attention. Sometimes, a story detail is worth a full scene. Sometimes, it's okay to sprinkle in a little summary, as we'll see in Chapter 9. Yes, this can even apply to character.

However, you shouldn't *only* tell about the entirety of a character, especially your protagonist. Explanation of

---

1. Well, you *can*. You can do whatever you want. But you wouldn't be well served by taking such an expository approach.

character is the precise "bad telling" we're talking about, because it's downright boring and one-dimensional to try and boil an entire human (or animal or creature or robot) down into a few attributes. Here are some bad examples:

> She was a nervous girl.

> He lied so much he couldn't keep track of the truth anymore.

> She was their commander, but she got that position through fear, not actual leadership.

When you explain anything, you are taking away from the reader's enjoyment of your work. And sometimes, that's fine. Readers appreciate knowing certain kinds of information more than they want to go digging for it. Sometimes, summary is the easiest, quickest, and most effective way to introduce a story element. But when it comes to character traits, theme, and scene dynamics, you're best off treading carefully and making the most intentional choices possible.

Let's consider a hypothetical situation. Imagine you're going to a friend's office party as a plus-one. You don't know any of the people there and might be a bit nervous to meet so many new faces. Let's also say your friend does a brief rundown of the usual suspects who'll be there in order to prepare you.

"Chris is a real loose cannon. You never know what he's going to say. And Susan is just the sweetest," you're told.

If you're looking for a low-key night, you might then gravitate toward Susan. But if you want a shot of unpredictable energy, you'll seek out Chris. This is all fine and good … if your friend has identified her co-workers correctly.

But what if you show up and Chris greets you with a warm hug and asks you about yourself, while Susan ices you out with one-word answers? Or maybe Susan is already three espresso martinis deep and pulls you up on top of a table to dance?

If your friend hadn't prepared you ahead of time, you might come away with the impression that Chris is sweet and Susan is either cold or out of control, respectively.

This is similar to telling about character in a number of ways. First, when the writer explains a character, we're getting the author's perspective, which is going to be biased. (In most cases, a writer will give good characters a generous description—because they're their ingenues and brainchildren—while tearing down the villains.) The telling is, therefore, already slanted through the writer's lens.

Second, a reader is always going to trust their interpretation of events more than anything they're told, as I mentioned in the previous chapter, and this especially goes for characterizations. So if we're told that Chris is wild and Susan is nice, but we bond with Chris while being turned off by Susan, whose take will be more valid? Ours or our friend's?

Sure, maybe the buddy who invited us to the party knows these people better or is used to seeing them in a work—rather than a party—context. Their evaluation might be valid. But I'm going to guess that when you remember your time at the celebration, you'll remember *your* experience of Chris and Susan, rather than deferring to what you've been told.

Third, actions are much more powerful than descriptions when it comes to character. We're *told* that Chris is "a loose cannon" and that Susan is "sweet," but when Chris talks to us for half an hour, seeming engaged and asking lots of questions, we might feel seen and validated in his presence. And when Susan tries to pull us up on a table, we rear back and get out of her way (unless we're looking to let loose, too). We remember how these people made us feel through their actions much more than we remember how they're described by a third party, even one we trust.

Fourth, characters can act in certain ways for their own ends, which we'll talk about more later in this guide. What if Chris is a predator and only plays the nice guy at parties to lure unsuspecting people in? If we've come to hold him in high regard, we might end up being unpleasantly surprised.

Finally, we might be especially dubious of a character who attempts to describe themselves. If Chris comes out of the gate claiming to be "the nice guy" and Susan shouts that she's "the party girl," our BS detectors might activate, even if Chris and Susan seem to be playing to type. What kind of person typifies and labels themselves? If you're anything like me, you might watch Chris and Susan extra closely as the evening unfolds for any signs of cracks in their respective façades.

Humans (and therefore characters) are chock-full of cognitive biases. For example, the "halo effect": a positive impression of a person, product, or company along one metric tends to extend to an overall positive impression, which makes people disregard reality. (The "horn effect" is the opposite. If we're told, per the above, that Chris is a troublemaker, this shadow might impact our impression of him until we get to know him better. In an office party setting, though, that kind of deep interaction is unlikely, so we leave with an incomplete or flat-out wrong read on Chris.)

So what we can take for granted as *facts* or *truth* or *reality* is incredibly malleable when it comes to characterizing details, people, impressions, and judgments. Irrefutable facts are better left for the hard sciences. In the art of personality and characterization, everything is biased, and your mission, if you choose to accept it, is to realize this and mold your reader's interpretation of your fictional (or real-life-based memoir) characters with the above in mind.

An obvious example of manipulating a character's effect on readers is the unreliable narrator, defined in the previous chapter, or the author who is intentionally misdirecting the audience for a clear storytelling purpose.

Let's say your book features random chapters from a mysterious POV character who doesn't seem connected to the rest of the story. But by inhabiting their heads, readers develop a soft spot for them—only to realize they've been reading the antagonist's perspective this entire time. This leaves audiences with a complex experience. They've developed feelings for the villain, have maybe even related to them. And *bam*! The bleeding-heart animal lover whose childhood trauma backstory they've been privy to has just blown up Gotham. What a gut punch! If done effectively, this kind of twist can really add a layer of the unexpected to a story.

Sometimes characters are figuring *themselves* out as the story unfolds and taking readers along for the ride. Just as audiences try to understand the protagonist, their worldview, and the backstory, characters are also actively discovering themselves while making meaning from the stories they're in.

In fact, here's an excerpt from the upmarket speculative novel, *When Women Were Dragons* by Kelly Barnhill, where the POV character, Alex, is combing her memories to make a decision about how she feels and what she believes. Since we're in her interiority, we get to see the process of manipulation firsthand:

> Did my father love my mother? To this day I can't say for sure. Most of the time, I don't believe he did. But in this moment, when I try to pin it in my memory,

> when I try to observe it for long enough so I can write
> it down, I think he … *yes*. I think, in that moment, as he
> held her, as he carried her, he loved her deeply.[i]

There's obviously a difficult family dynamic in play, but here, we can witness Alex questioning her impressions, interpreting a memory, and then choosing how to move forward. It's a powerful expression of just how malleable the past can be, and how it can be shaped into a narrative that a protagonist either wants or needs to believe in order to proceed through the plot.

There's more to characterization than the broadest possible strokes. In fact, most protagonists and nuanced characters are artful combinations of key storytelling components. Here's an overview of craft elements you can use to create a deep impression of any character, but especially your POV protagonist:

- Action (showing);
- Dialogue (showing);
- Sense of Self (showing and telling);
- Objective and Motivation (showing and telling);
- Backstory (showing and telling);
- Worldview (showing and telling);
- Need (mostly telling); and
- Inner Struggle (mostly telling).

Let's talk about action and dialogue first, as you are likely most comfortable with those if you've been closely following the "show, don't tell" advice.

Action (Showing)

First and foremost, you can and should convey characters in action. This is classic showing, and it absolutely has a place in storytelling, even if we *also* push into some good telling. Think about Katniss from *The Hunger Games* by Suzanne Collins. She's notoriously prickly and standoffish. But then she volunteers to go to—and potentially die in—the Hunger Games in order to save her sister. For all of the other negative impressions Katniss makes on readers and other characters, her actions give her away as someone who cares deeply about the things and people who matter to her.

This is, actually, the entire foundation of the Save the Cat[2] methodology, which suggests you should have a character showcase their softer or more vulnerable side right away to get readers on their team.

Action strips away bias and leaves readers to make the purest interpretation possible—their read of what a character is doing and what the underlying motivations might be. We've all heard the old maxim that actions speak louder than words. When it comes to characters telling about themselves (or others), this is doubly true. Rather than hearing summary that attempts to wrap a character into a neat little package—the bad kind of telling—we want to get to know them ourselves.

What they do, how they do it, and the circumstances surrounding the action are powerful tools for portraying a protagonist or secondary character's goals, motivations, worldviews, values, priorities, and more. If a character rallies their school with an anti-bullying campaign but trash-talks his best friend behind their back, there's a disconnect for readers to interpret. Is he a justice warrior or a morally gray opportunist?

As with many of these other tools for showcasing character,

---

2. This originated with Blake Snyder's *Save The Cat! The Last Book on Screenwriting You'll Ever Need*, then was adapted into *Save the Cat Writes a Novel* by Jessica Brody.

actions can be used to manipulate and mislead. The villain saves the cat from a storm drain only because there's a newspaper reporter taking pictures. An older sibling shares with their younger brother because they know the parents are watching and want dessert that night. An employee starts logging on during the weekend and on evenings … in the weeks before the quarterly performance review.

But in general, action is the most direct line to triggering reader interpretation because audiences know to activate their detective brains when they see a character in motion. Whether they're being led or misled, their own opinions of and reactions to what they're reading are going to be on high alert as the scene unfolds.

Dialogue (Showing)

One step below action on the purity of interpretation ladder (this term doesn't quite roll off the tongue!) is dialogue. It shares a lot in common with action in that it's the external demonstration of what a character might have going on inside them. Therefore, it does a good job of conveying who the character might be.

However, while action can be faked for selfish purposes and to sway readers and in-story observers, dialogue tends to suffer from a magnified version of the same problem. After all, we often act and speak differently in different situations and to different people in our lives. Characters are the same.

Think about the last time you tried to sweet-talk someone to get what you wanted. It doesn't have to be nefarious, but it happens. Or if you've ever been cordial to someone's face, then quickly gotten on your group chat with your best friends to complain about the same individual. (This might reveal more about who you are than it does about the person you're discussing!)

A wonderful example of this type of masking is demonstrated throughout *James* by Percival Everett. In that historical novel, which dramatizes Jim's perspective from *Huckleberry Finn* by Mark Twain, the enslaved Black people speak in a broken pidgin English whenever white characters are around, but are expressive and fully in command of their rhetoric whenever they're among their own. In the time of slavery, this is a survival strategy.

There are a few close calls, as readers know how dangerous it is for enslaved people to reveal they're equal or superior to white people in this era, and we'll see this excerpted in Chapter 10. Masking also ends up playing a role in Jim's relationship to Huck when Jim reveals his true self to the boy as a sign of vulnerability and friendship. Huck is surprised and hurt that Jim would hide this facet of himself but eventually understands the cultural forces which made Jim alter his behavior according to his circumstances.

Consider how your character speaks when they're being truly themselves versus the dialogue, voice, and tone they'll use when they're pretending. As such, readers might take dialogue with a grain of salt when forming their interpretations of character. If dialogue and action match up, that's a more compelling way to convey who someone is—or who they're trying to be.

A writer's first instinct when heartily applying "show, don't tell" might be to throw necessary story information into dialogue. Because speaking is showing, right? I understand the thinking behind this move. Dialogue is, after all, external. It's technically happening in action, in that it takes place in the present moment, with characters doing other scene-relevant business. The interactivity between your cast members makes the pacing move along more quickly.

But telling in narration and telling between quotation marks are exactly the same. One is just sneakier. Don't get me wrong, you get cutie pie points for being so clever, smart, and beautiful. Alas, many of the same problems we see with telling are also affecting your work when you're couching information in dialogue, which is *literal* telling (since they're talking).

You can certainly present data this way—also called "expository dialogue"—to contextualize a scene, the present action, a character or relationship, the past (discussing it) and future (speculating, hoping, or worrying about it), and more.

However, you don't want characters explaining themselves, as we saw in the previous chapter. And you'll want to make the dialogue organic. The worst kind of telling in dialogue has a fun nickname in creative writing circles: "As You Know, Bob."

It goes something like this:

> "As you know, Bob, we grew up together, so I care about you. And I'm worried that this heist is going to turn you into a different person. Someone I don't recognize anymore."

Here, the speaker is reminding Bob of their shared history and explaining the present situation. There's some attempt at emotion and action—this character is worried they'll lose Bob if he changes his value system—but it's entirely unnatural to sit around and tell a shared situation (or backstory) to one another.

And, in case there's any lingering doubt, you should absolutely not tell using fancy "said" synonyms or adverbs in dialogue tags. Avoid "she joked" and "he exclaimed proudly." This is the kind of basic bad telling that marks many aspiring manuscripts as amateur. The trick is to make the dialogue speak for itself in voice, paired with the reader's understanding of the character and story context. The pride in the above example should be clear without you having to name it.

Dialogue is, of course, instrumental in storytelling, and we'll talk more about scene in Chapter 9. Crucially, action and dialogue are our main avenues for learning about characters when we don't have point-of-view access to them, because we don't benefit from knowing their interiority (we'll discuss this in Chapter 7). So use these tools intentionally and consider how your characters might come across based on their dialogue.

Finally, it's important to remember that readers will invariably bring their own impressions and biases to the page, so you'll never be able to perfectly steer them to your desired characterization. Just read some book reviews to see this in action. Some audiences might love sweet, patient office-party Chris, who makes them feel like they're the only person in the room. Others might find him clingy. Some audiences will be turned off by martini-glugging Susan, while others might think she seems fun (and that everyone else is stuck-up).

We'll read more examples of telling, showing, and dialogue in Chapter 9, when we talk about what to render in summary versus scene. In the following chapter, let's pivot to other characterizing elements that are both shown and told, like a protagonist's sense of self, objective, and motivation.

4

SENSE OF SELF, OBJECTIVE, AND MOTIVATION

The following two craft concepts (sense of self and objective/motivation) peel back the superficial showing layer of action and dialogue to enter the domain of both showing *and* telling as it pertains to characterization.

Sense of Self (Showing and Telling)

I devoted an entire chapter of *Writing Interiority* to the idea of a POV protagonist's sense of self, but here, I'll stick primarily to how sense of self can be told. The truth is, identities are complicated, and characters don't always present themselves in straightforward ways. While it is perfectly possible to show sense of self—Katniss volunteering to potentially give up her life for her sister, how a character talks to or acts toward someone, etc.—you're going to have a tougher time fully exploring identity without *some* telling.

There's nothing straightforward about the process of conveying this on the page. That said, readers will be curious about a few things, first and foremost, which all benefit from some telling:

CHAPTER 4

- Who does the character believe themselves to be?
- What does the character think *about* that self?
- Are they poised for a growth arc or are they mostly happy with who they are?
- If the character wants to grow or evolve, what do they want to change about themselves?
- Do they reveal their true self to *others*? Does that vulnerability cost them anything? If they don't, why not?
- Do they reveal their true self to *themselves*? Does that vulnerability cost them anything? If they don't, why not?

Of course, you want to be careful about telling *everything* here, lest your character gets in the habit of sitting around philosophizing about themselves or explaining who they are to readers.

Outside the walls of therapist's office or rehab, we're not often baring our souls to other people or expressing what makes us tick in a straightforward way. Sure, we can do this with our intimates—people we know and feel comfortable being vulnerable around—but those conversations are almost *less* likely to feature characters explaining themselves to one another. They're good for hashing out relationship dynamics and tracking change over time, but not for establishing the basics.

When's the last time you met someone in a casual setting, maybe for the first time, who said something like:

> "You know, the reason I tend to keep people at arm's length when I first start dating them is because my father left us. I've had trouble trusting that I won't be abandoned ever since."

Or:

> "People call me ambitious, but, really, I'm driven by deep insecurity. My parents only paid attention to my brother when he was winning track and field medals. When he died in that car accident, I knew I had to do everything in my power to achieve for the both of us. Too bad they don't see it that way. No matter what I do, my parents don't care because I'm not him."

Sure, we learn some backstory, need, and wound information, but there's no finesse, nuance, intention, or artistry to how it's expressed.

It's also incredibly inorganic, which is a bit more of a moving target, as everyone has a different understanding of and threshold for verisimilitude. I cannot imagine a human saying this in earnest to another human. If someone said something like this as soon as they sat down next to me on an airplane, I would probably activate the over-wing slide.

For me, or maybe them. I'm not sure yet.

People do not talk this way. And not just because it's vulnerable and too on-the-nose. In fact, some people—and, by extension, characters—are not self-aware enough to realize these kinds of things about themselves. At least maybe not until later in their own stories.

If a character has it all figured out—their wound, need, character arc, and the reasons for any foibles or misbeliefs— they are too perfect. There's no room for mess or reality or growth. Readers are less likely to engage because the characters don't resemble us, know everything already, and simply explain themselves to audiences. This type of characterization can be interesting if the character asserts one thing but does another or is ironically (or unironically) wrong about their self-assessment. Then we scratch at the surface of inner struggle.

That said, there's still something powerful about character self-evaluation and assessment, as long as it feels real. We all think and talk about ourselves, analyze our personalities (or try not to, which is a characterizing detail in and of itself), and maintain a daily relationship with our deeper identity.

It's okay to tell certain things, especially if a character is having a turning point moment where they're using interiority at the extrapolation ("What does this mean *for* me?") or subsummation ("What does this mean *about* me?") levels to unpack and react to whatever's happening internally or externally.

Here are some examples of characters telling about themselves. We would not have much of the richness we're about to explore, below, without some component of telling, as it's impossible to show all of these ideas in action without an underlying peek into what's going on in each character's head.

Our first example is from the upmarket novel *How to Age Disgracefully* by Claire Pooley, as a downtrodden character named Lydia considers her external (social) identity, represented by her various names, and how little it seems to correlate to who she feels she is inside:

> Then she'd given up her surname. Followed, when the girls arrived, by her job. And she'd even stopped being referred to as Lydia much of the time. She was "Mummy" or "Darling" or "Mrs. Roberts." Sometimes she lost any form of name at all, and became just an adjunct: "Sophia's Mum," or "Jeremy's Plus-One." When she pictured scenes from the past,

she felt like the Lydia she was looking at was a
completely different person. She couldn't remember
what it felt like to be her.[i]

This novel is largely about midlife and beyond, as characters
grapple with who they are, who they were, and who they're
becoming in their golden years. It assembles a cast of very
different characters in an ensemble of alternating POVs. Some
of the narrators are self-possessed and know themselves
deeply. Others, like Lydia, have room to grow. This excerpt
positions us at the beginning of her development arc so
readers can then chart who she becomes over the course of
the story. This is a great use of telling—you can have a
character provide self-assessment at the beginning of their
journey, around the midpoint, and then toward the end,
especially if your work has strong themes of personal
development, as this one does.

In an example of late character transformation, we meet Jude,
who is completely unmoored at the conclusion of the YA
fantasy thriller *The Invocations* by Krystal Sutherland. In her
case, this might not actually be a bad thing, as Jude has spent
the entire narrative trying to get out from under her father's
financial, emotional, and even paranormal control:

Jude does not know what to do with the vastness
of it. Who is she, now? Who is she now that everyone
is dead? Grief and relief crash together inside her.[ii]

Notice that we're naming emotions ("grief and relief crash
together") and offering a straightforward statement of
confusion: "Jude does not know what to do with the
vastness of it." However, this also invites readers to interpret
that she's not entirely terrified and sees new opportunities
ahead of her—represented by the open-ended rhetorical
questions.

The next excerpt, from *Midnight Is the Darkest Hour* by Ashley Winstead, a Southern gothic thriller, features Ruth explaining herself to readers. Hers is a first-person POV, though you wouldn't know it from this sample:

> If you were to ask around about Miss Ruth Cornier, you'd hear the same story: Miss Ruth Cornier, they'd tell you, is a good God-fearing girl, not a lick of trouble, raised by two upstanding, cane-wielding pillars of the community. But [she's] intensely shy to the point of muteness, to the point of not being able to function when spoken to, a girl who grows red-faced and stuttering upon too forward a glance. A wisp of a girl, someone who haunts the background of photographs, unlikely to look a boy in the eyes, let alone date one.[iii]

Fans of anything Southern-inflected will love the "folksy" storytelling voice. Oddly, though, this is Ruth talking about herself in the third person. She's shy and retiring, so this "outside-in" perspective, while unusual for first-person POV, where "inside-out" is the main draw, makes sense. She's the daughter of a preacher and must watch herself closely … which is also why this choice resonates on a deeper level. She's so highly attuned to how others judge her that it has leeched into her own self-perception.

On the other hand, characters can also define themselves by their highest impulses, as Orkideh does in the literary novel *Martyr!* by Kaveh Akbar. She is an artist and has a complicated relationship to her work (as we all do), where she defines herself through her art and her art through herself. This lens is incredibly illuminating to readers, who are trying to learn more about her, as she has been somewhat of a mystery—with infrequent POV chapters—for most of the story:

Every time I finish something, still, I am certain it's the best thing I've ever made, that everything else was the useful disposable compost preparing my living for the masterpiece I've just wrought. Painting saved me, but I can't say I loved painting. I painted because I needed to. What I really loved, what I love, is having-painted. That was the high. Making something that would never have existed in the entirety of humanity had I not been there at that specific moment to make it. I resented work for this reason more than any other. The countless paintings that would never exist because I had to be working for money instead of painting. I resented my body for the same reasons, its ravenous gobbling up of time, its constant calibrations, needing to eat, shit, smoke.[iv]

Relatable, no? I also frequently hate writing, while I love having written. The novel's twist reveal at the end is all about how this artist is connected to the protagonist. After reading this, audiences can go into the climax having understood her deepest essence.

Here's another take on a protagonist's relationship to art, though this one tracks a downward trajectory. It's from the upmarket novel *The Wedding People* by Alison Espach and offers context for Phoebe, a recent divorcée who has unintentionally crashed a wedding by showing up at a fully booked hotel where she'd planned to die by suicide. The wedding surprises her, and she surprises everyone there with her dark intentions:

Phoebe used to read books and feel astounded. She used to walk around galleries, inspired by the beautiful human urge to create. But that was years ago. Now she can't stand the sight of her books. Can't bear the thought of reading hundreds of pages just to watch Jane Eyre get married again.[v]

While we see Phoebe becoming disenchanted with literature here, probably because of her own recent midlife crisis, this summary telling offers a window of what recovery might look like. Will Phoebe be restored to her true sense of self when she's able to pick up a book and enjoy it again?[1] The telling doesn't just offer a fact about the character. It gives readers a sense of the past *and* potential future.

The key is noticing *how* this is done. The author doesn't say, "While Phoebe used to love reading, she couldn't stand it anymore. All those happy endings left a bitter taste in her mouth after her divorce. If only she could one day find this version of herself again." Compare that to what's actually been written. My version is flat, explanatory. It leaves readers no room for interpretation. The published version invites a reader to make meaning.

Up next is another portrait of a character self-evaluating her personality, also while on a downward swing. This comes from the upmarket *Blue Sisters* by Coco Mellors, as the ironically named Lucky hits a rough patch. She not only tells readers how she feels about herself, but what her nearest and dearest think of her (though this is, of course, a biased interpretation, based on how ashamed she is at the moment). Here, she's in the midst of hitting rock bottom, and her way of coping is to wallow in her shame:

> She'd heard once that guilt was for something you'd done—you could feel guilty for a certain behavior or action but still fundamentally know you were a good person—but shame was deeper, shame

---

1. Spoiler alert: This is one of the final images of the novel.

was for who you were. Lucky didn't simply do bad things, she *was* bad, she saw that now. If the real her came out when she drank, then the real her was clearly a nightmare. She was like some vicious, snarling animal caught in a trap, swiping at the hand that tried to help. No one who had seen her last night, or on any of the hundreds of nights she'd been drunk the past few years, would want anything to do with her. And now not even her sisters would either. Avery already hated her, and after last night, Bonnie would too. She had no one.[vi]

Will Lucky stay in this funk? Probably not. This is the Dark Night of the Soul moment (see more on this in Chapter 8), and it's usually a launching pad for the character's eventual triumph or evolution. Like the previous *The Wedding People* example, it leaves room for the character to grow and invites readers to root for her and imagine what her next steps might look like.

We'll wrap up this section with an excerpt from the literary novel *Trust* by Hernan Diaz. Here, Benjamin realizes his entire self-concept was incomplete until he found his missing piece —a companion. We'll talk more about showing and telling as they pertain to secondary characters in Chapter 7, but this sample tackles a protagonist's interpretation of self when someone else enters their orbit. Only once he's met a mate does he have occasion to completely reevaluate what he thought he knew about himself:

> Intimacy can be an unbearable burden for those who, first experiencing it after a lifetime of proud self-sufficiency, suddenly realize it makes their world complete. Finding bliss becomes one with the fear of losing it. They doubt their right to hold someone else accountable for their happiness; they worry that their

loved one may find their reverence tedious; they fear their yearning may have distorted their features in ways they cannot see. Thus, as the weight of all these questions and concerns bends them inward, their newfound joy in companionship turns into a deeper expression of the solitude they thought they had left behind.[vii]

This is a fascinating passage, told in a heightened literary voice, which projects Benjamin's experience onto an imagined generic "they." It explores the duality of being a solitary creature in relationship with another person. The highs and the lows of love aren't explained here—they are considered thoughtfully. We go into the protagonist's interiority as Benjamin rides the razor's edge between being alone and being reliant on someone else.

This excerpt also hints at another crucial component of a character's expression of self: what they want. Objective (their desire) and motivation (their reasoning) are, after all, the craft elements that initially put lot of protagonists into action and vaunt them into showing. But all of that external activity would be meaningless without some context and supportive telling.

Objective and Motivation (Showing and Telling)

If you've read any of my other writing guides, you know I'm a sucker for giving the protagonist a strong objective and motivation, early and often. The reasoning behind this is simple: You want to create a proactive character who's capable of changing their lot in life for the better (especially if they're unhappy, as they often are before they launch into the story proper during the inciting incident). There's almost no better way to get readers invested in a character's potential, as well as to hint at a juicy development trajectory to come, than by putting them into action in the service of a goal.

An objective is what a character wants. Their motivation is why they want it. Of course, when it comes to creating multi-layered protagonists, there's a lot more that goes into it, like the wound and need (which we'll talk about in the following chapter). The objective likely came from somewhere, as did the motivation. The character might have a belief or value system that informs their desires, which they either arrived at randomly (unlikely) or which was influenced by the context of their family of origin, early experiences, culture, society, religious or faith tradition, etc., etc., etc. This is encapsulated in their backstory, which we'll discuss in Chapter 5 as well.

Why do we want what we want? Is it nature or nurture? There generally isn't just one clear-cut answer to these questions, but this is the fertile ground you're playing in when you decide to develop your protagonist.

There are a few complicating factors, however. Like characters, objectives and motivations can change. In fact, they tend to have their own arc. This is a wild generalization, but a protagonist tends to transition from pursuing their objective and "trying to solve the problem the wrong way" to trying to "solving the problem the right way" and pursue their deeper need around the midpoint. This doesn't have to be the exact 50% mark in the manuscript, of course, but as the character gains more experience in tackling their specific conflicts and plot while weathering both internal and external struggles, they might decide their objective, which is often driven by some kind of shortsightedness or misbelief to begin with, isn't cutting it anymore.

They need to look their need and wound head-on and take steps to shed light on and/or heal *those* instead, at least if they want the life they've always envisioned, dreamed of, or hoped for. But that's a problem for another chapter (Chapter 6, in fact!). First, we need to establish their initial objective and motivation. The sooner the better, too, so they can hit the ground running, ideally in your first few scenes, and are shown to be go-getters in motion, even if what they're pursuing isn't going to end up being their ultimate endgame.

So how do we introduce objective and motivation while keeping an eye on good telling and showing? Well, sometimes we can simply state these attributes. Easy-peasy, mac-and-cheesy.

Here are some examples from the shelves of compelling objective and motivation statements. Our first is a straightforward expression of want, which many readers in this book's target demographic might relate to. This is an unnamed[2] protagonist from *Crush* by Ada Calhoun, a typical overworked mother coming up on middle age, who feels the spark has gone out of her life:

> While it was true that I never complained about how much I was doing to keep food in the house and money in the bank, it was also true that I was exhausted. For my entire adult life I'd been working more than full time while cooking, cleaning, and handling all the chores that come with responsible adulthood. If I'd been approached by the devil at a crossroads, I would have asked for nothing more than a week alone with no errands.[viii]

Many women's fiction readers will resonate here. This isn't just a straightforward statement of objective, it also conveys the character's current lot in life, feeling about it, and

---

2. A veritable "Everywoman." This is an intentional choice, made, perhaps, to foster audience engagement.

worldview. She's overburdened, and all she wants is a break. The fantasy of having a week without any errands also suggests that such an idea, from where she's sitting, seems preposterous. (If it felt feasible to her, she'd maybe aim a bit higher with her objective.) So while we get telling in this excerpt, and it's relatively on-the-nose, there's still something for readers to interpret.

Up next, we see an example of the intersection of identity and want for Sadie, from the literary novel *Tomorrow, and Tomorrow, and Tomorrow* by Gabrielle Zevin:

> Recently, she had suspected he was losing interest in her. So, she had attempted to make herself more interesting. She had tried to dress better, and she'd gotten a haircut and she bought lacy underwear. She had read a book about wine, so she could be knowledgeable at dinner, the way she imagined an older lover would be…. But it didn't seem to matter.[ix]

This is a superficial statement of objective. Sadie doesn't necessarily want to become more interesting for her own purposes. She wants to be seen as more interesting by Dov, her lover, in order to save a failing relationship.

Up next is a character, Opal, who we already met in the previous chapter, from *Starling House* by Alix E. Harrow. In this scene, she confronts Arthur, a mysterious young man she's managed to befriend, about what she wants. Then she layers on what this might mean about her sense of identity in interiority:

> "I want—"
> The truth is I want him and I'm scared of wanting him and ashamed of being scared. The truth is I'm a coward and a liar and a cold bastard, just like my

mother, and in the end I will let him drown to save
myself. I should cut and run right now, before it's too
late, before he finds out what kind of person I
really am.[x]

Opal has been fending for herself for as long as she's been
alive, working a dead-end job and staying in a motel with a
neglectful mother. When she meets Arthur, who lives in the
mysterious (and potentially alive) Starling House, she
reevaluates everything she believes about herself, as the
protagonist of *Trust*, Benjamin, did in the previous section.

Here, we weave telling about sense of self together with what
Opal wants. Except she already knows her objective—Arthur
—is superficial because she's considering how she might use
him. These statements seem simple at face value, but there's a
lot of depth to interpret, leaving something for readers to do.
Is Opal certain she's "a coward and a liar and a cold bastard,
just like [her] mother," or is she merely scared this is the case
because she's never actually expressed feelings or desire for
anyone else before? Maybe Arthur won't prove the worst
things she believes about herself, and instead, he'll be an
opportunity to rise above these deep insecurities and
vulnerabilities. Thus, objective is another opportunity for
readers to learn about a character's inner struggle.

The above passage also introduces the idea that sometimes a
character shouldn't want what they, in fact, do. Where does
this come from? It can certainly originate with worldview and
past experience. Maybe we don't realize we should and/or
can want and/or have nice things because of an ideology
bred into us that we should never try to rise above our
station. Like Lucky from *Blue Sisters* in the previous section, a
character might believe they are bad and therefore unworthy.
Or we tell ourselves we want X, when we really need Y. We'll
explore this some more in Chapter 6.

Here's a teaser example of a character telling us what she "wants" … yet it makes the unmistakable impression that she really does need something else. This passage comes from the thriller *You Can't Hurt Me* by Emma Cook, as Anna discusses her dating life:

> "Superficial dating never hurts anyone," I say defensively. Tinder was perfect. Fleeting, transient, under the radar. My love life had been much more manageable this way, skimming the surfaces and avoiding the depths. "Here's to never being hurt again," I said, raising a glass.[xi]

Here, Anna is telling us what she wants directly, but she's lying. To herself, her conversation partners in the scene, *and* to readers.

Let's continue with a similarly delusional passage. The next character, Natalia, from *City of Night Birds* by Juhea Kim, wants too much. She's a former competitive ballerina who has spent her entire life in the pursuit of artistic excellence. In this scene, she gets drunk and considers what life might look like if she stopped chasing her dream:

> And somewhere between my second and third glass, I realize how possible it is to give up and accept defeat. How pleasant, even. I have nothing to prove to anyone—I don't have to *be* anything. I used to look down on people whose only objective in life is going to work, coming home, eating dinner, watching a show, and going to bed, and now their simple satisfaction in the mundane seems to signify maturity and wisdom. Tomorrow, I will book the next flight out of Piter … pack up the furniture in my apartment in Paris, buy a cheap place in the country, find some regular routine. Live quietly until the money runs out

—which should not be for at least several years. I can't picture what happens next, but again that's asking too much of myself for no reason. I've lived my entire life as though swimming upriver, and now I'm ready for the lovely, whole surrender of letting the current carry me down. My mind thus made up, I fall into a dreamless, unmedicated sleep for the first time in months.[xii]

This sample also gets at the difference between objective and need. Maybe she thinks she wants an entirely different life, but what she really needs is to stop running herself ragged and allow herself to relax in her present circumstances. That, of course, is very difficult for a person like her, which this passage does a great job of conveying without overt explanation. Yes, this *is* telling, as the narrator is offering readers a statement of fact. But the audience must unpack this information in order for the protagonist to emerge clearly in their mind's eye.

Another character from *Blue Sisters* by Coco Mellors, Bonnie, tackles the same idea of drive and desire, only this time, it's about her passion for competitive boxing:

Most people go through life never knowing what it's like to have a calling, one that asks you to sacrifice the pleasure of the moment for the potential of a dream that may not be realized for years, if at all. It sets you apart from others, whether you want it to or not. It can be grueling, lonely, and punishing, but, if it is really your calling, it is not a choice.[xiii]

Notice how complicated each character's relationship to their life's objective is. The last two protagonists both seem to speak as if their craft is a foregone conclusion, not a choice. Of course, they can both stop, but they don't. Or won't. And the fact that they don't, even as they're suffering, tells readers something else about their personalities.

We're back to Phoebe from *The Wedding People* by Alison Espach for another excerpt. Here, she wishes she could stop Gary and Lila's wedding after realizing she has caught feelings for Gary. Notice how her own desires influence her thinking. Remember, protagonist perspectives are biased. As she guesses what might've happened between Gary and his fiancée, Lila, the night before the wedding—a make-or-break point in the story—her own wants are in the foreground:

> [Phoebe] wishes she could know what happened last night with Gary after he left … Did Lila confess to having a crush on Jim and did Gary confess to having a crush on Phoebe and did their confessions somehow make them stronger, the way confessions usually do? Or did they say nothing at all? Did they just hold their hands and smile at each other and proceed forward like normal?[xiv]

Sometimes a character's stated desire is magical thinking—that Gary will call the wedding off and be with Phoebe. Readers are then invited to extrapolate what this might mean. We already know Phoebe is a fan of classic literature who has lost her passion for reading. And yet, given the above, could it be that she's holding out a tiny sliver of hope for her own happy ending? Telling is about what you say, and what a character says, but also about what is left unsaid, allowing readers to connect the dots you're planting or come to their own conclusions.

And then there are the characters who don't know what they want, which can contribute to a lot of inner struggle and plot conflict to a story, too. In *When Women Were Dragons* by Kelly Barnhill, the world very much acts upon Alex, instead of the other way around. She's a young woman, and women in this world (suburban 1950s America) are feeling so put-upon and oppressed that they literally become dragons and take to the sky, which is this story's speculative element. Alex's aunt has become a dragon, and her niece (who everyone pretends is her sister), Beatrice, might be heading in the same direction. Where does that leave her? Through telling readers that she doesn't know what direction her life will take, Alex is metabolizing her own sense of uncertainty and giving audiences a launching pad from which to imagine what the future of the story might be:

> My future after graduation was a yawning space. What would happen to us? How could I continue to raise Beatrice while I continued my education? I knew I needed to have both, I knew that they both were *necessary*, but how it would work was a mystery. I had no context to even begin to imagine it ... it was a hole in the universe where the truth should be, and where my life would be.
>
> And, frankly, I was afraid.
>
> When I was a little girl, they told us to keep our eyes on the ground. They told us not to ask about the houses that burned. They told us to forget ...
>
> And now I realize, there is a freedom in forgetting.
>
> Or at least it is something that feels like freedom.
>
> There is a freedom in *not* asking questions.
>
> There is a freedom in being unburdened by unpleasant information.
>
> And sometimes, a person has to hang on to whatever freedoms she can get.[xv]

A choice is implied within these statements. She says she wants to be "free" (even if it is an attenuated type of freedom) from the truth through denial, yet she's approaching a crossroads where she will have to take a stand and decide what she believes. Freedom might have felt safe once upon a time, but Alex no longer has that luxury because childhood is ending and the rest of her life is coming, whether she likes it or not. This excerpt also introduces a quick burst of backstory —or foundational information about a character's past.

As we continue our exploration of how telling establishes foundational character craft concepts, we'll dig into backstory and worldview in the following chapter.

5

BACKSTORY AND WORLDVIEW

In the seminal book, *Thinking, Fast and Slow*, Daniel Kahneman summarizes that people have two primary mental modes of existence: the "experiencing self" and the "remembering self."

For the most part, your POV character is living through the story in the present moment (even if you're writing in past tense, most of the narrative will be conveyed *as it's happening* to the character), which is the "experiencing self." And this is where the majority of your plot, character expectation, reaction, and interiority will dwell.

But sometimes you'll need to step out of time to fill in the past (either through summary or full scene), or reflect on those events and make meaning from them. This is where we get into the "remembering self." The issue with the remembering self, however, is that all kinds of cognitive biases come into play once a character has some distance from an event. Memories are tinged with a protagonist's emotion about the situation, their perception of the other characters involved, and their knowledge of the outcome. Once the experience passes, a character can also apply hindsight and reflection.

Writers *and* readers must keep in mind that recollections are merely a snapshot of a character's impression of a past event, recalled in the present moment. If they're having a fight with their best friend, they might regret first meeting that person: "I rue the day." But if the friends reconcile, this can go back to being a cherished memory, part of their mutual lore.

Once we understand the past is biased and only as good as the mood of the person telling it in the current timeline, we must also consider how to present backstory in the most effective way possible, so as not to impact the pacing of the present narrative. Whenever you offer information, a story's momentum and forward progress suffers. As such, backstory needs to be introduced with a careful hand, so as not to overwhelm readers or stall the plot.

In many of my editorial practice and IP development projects, I'm struck by the question of how, exactly, to get backstory into the work without explaining it *or* putting it into dialogue. Readers often need a lot of data in order to fully understand your character. This information might have to do with their wound or need, the secondary relationships in their lives (especially with characters who were foundational to their development), significant locations from their upbringing, or events that have shaped their philosophy and worldview.

This is especially relevant when we think about structuring the beginnings of our stories, because those opening chapters require the masterful inclusion of competing yet necessary ingredients. For example, you need to kick off the plot, but nobody is going to care about the action before they get to know your characters. You also need to introduce your protagonist, conflict and tension, dialogue and scene, other characters who bring out certain layers in your protagonist, a voice and distinct writing style, genre expectations and tropes (if relevant to your specific project), setting and world-building and … and … it's enough to make someone sign up for a root canal rather than subject themselves to the blood sport of first pages. Especially when me, and other writing teachers, tell them they can't, well, tell.

(Jokes aside, opening pages and chapters are so important to both storytelling and generating excitement for your project among readers and gatekeepers that I have—of course—written an entire separate book called *Writing Irresistible First Pages: How to Craft Compelling Story Openings That Will Hook Gatekeepers and Readers*.)

Here's actual footage of me in my office:

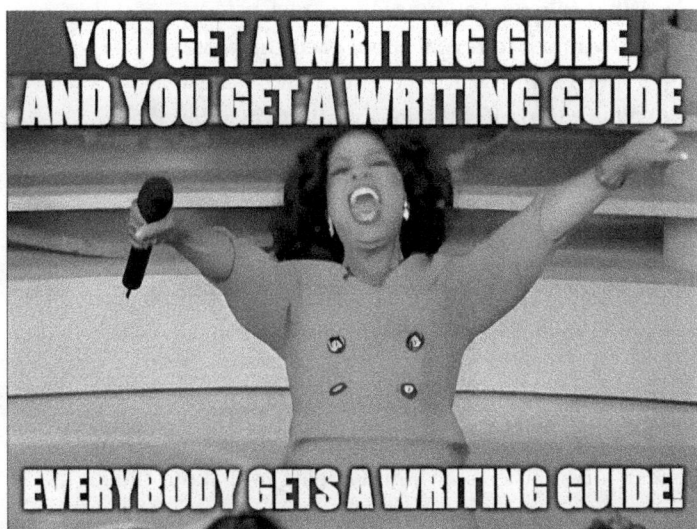

Okay, *now* I'm done with the jokes, and we can get back to our scheduled programming by digging deeper into backstory.

Backstory (Showing and Telling)

The truth is, sometimes it's simpler and cleaner to explain elements of a character's backstory, which is technically delivered either in summary or full flashback (giving a past event the complete scene treatment with setting description, dialogue, action, and interiority), which we'll talk about in Chapter 9. With both of these approaches, some telling is going to be expected and accepted.

It's then up to you to decide:

- What to reveal about each character;
- How much to reveal about each character;
- Where to introduce the information; and
- Whether to offer the information via telling and summary or full flashback.

The more important the backstory element is to the present action, the earlier it should come into play (unless you're reserving it for a climactic twist or reveal) and the more rendering it should get (a flashback scene as opposed to summary telling). Flashback scenes are also excellent for putting dead and otherwise unavailable characters on the page so readers can "meet" them and draw their own conclusions, rather than simply being told about them. Remember, with character especially, you don't want to lean entirely on telling/explanation (without *any* showing component) unless you absolutely can't get around it for some reason.[1]

---

1. The "for some reason" better be really compelling because, in fiction at least, you're making the whole damn thing up! If you realize you've written yourself into a brick wall, change the layout of the entire neighborhood. It's all within your control, and the only limitations are those you've placed on yourself. In memoir, it's a little trickier, but I strongly believe you can also find your way around most narrative dead ends by choosing to spotlight

Backstory about the protagonist is obviously more relevant and interesting to the story than the personal history of a character we meet for ten pages. It's also true that most writers won't end up using every single scrap of backstory they've developed for each of their characters. A lot of this data exists to inform the writer, rather than the reader, so the creator can have a fuller understanding of their protagonist and important secondary characters.

However, if you find yourself fascinated by your protagonist's backstory and dredging it up at the expense of your present plot, you might want to start your story earlier, as you are clearly drawn to another time period in the character's life. You can also consider narrating in multiple timelines to include fully realized dramatization of those previous events.

Not every moment in a protagonist's past will be created equal, either. Some backstory will be especially singular, traumatic, or formative. The character might be able to point to an event where their life split into a "before" and an "after," and there's no going back to who they were. This can be something sudden and tragic, like a car accident that killed their younger sibling, or something internal but still significant, like the choice they made to never talk to their father again after watching him slam Mom against the wall.

However, it's simplistic and reductive to pin a character's sense of self, wound, and need (the latter two are discussed a bit later) on *one thing*. All personalities are a combination of nature, nurture, and a million lived experiences—those remembered, misremembered, and even repressed.

---

different scenes or events, shifting the focus, or taking small creative liberties with the source material (combining two aunts into one, shifting the time of year, etc.), as long as you uphold the essence and purity of your perception of your experiences as faithfully as you can.

CHAPTER 5

Sometimes a character's backstory can emerge for readers from seemingly unrelated memories which provide a picture of their upbringing. For example, a car accident might be jarring and have a profound impact on a protagonist, but emotional neglect which quietly and insidiously sprawls across the entirety of their childhood can also have devastating effects. Sometimes it's a little from column A (several key past moments rendered in flashback) and a little from column B (summary telling about the overall atmosphere of a love-starved household).

Let's dive into some examples of good telling when it comes to backstory. Here's an early summary of Alex's experience in the big city from *The Guest* by Emma Cline. This story is a bit of an outlier, as Alex is an unreliable narrator. Her recollection is fuzzy—on purpose. She's not being forthcoming because she's ashamed. In fact, she goes so far as to enter complete delusion by the end of the novel:[2]

> [Alex had] been twenty when she first arrived in the city. Back when she still had the energy to use a fake name and still believed gestures like that had value, meant the things she was doing weren't actually happening in her real life. Back when she kept lists: The names of the places she went with the men. Restaurants that charged for bread and butter. Restaurants that refolded your napkin when you went to the bathroom. Restaurants that only served steak, pink but flavorless and thick as a hardcover book. Brunches at mid-range hotels, with unripe strawberries and too-sweet juice, slurry with pulp. But the appeal of

---

2. I did a comprehensive exploration of her character in *Writing Interiority* because this book offers a fascinating counterpoint to a more straightforward development arc. Though I tried not to reuse novels and excerpts from that guide, you'll see a few repeat works here. I just liked them too much!

the lists worse off quickly or something about them
started to depress her, so she stopped.[i]

Notice how Alex alludes to keeping records of the past (the
lists) but eventually ditches the habit. This information
reflects how she interfaces with her own life, erasing the
record so she can start over.

Sometimes an image can stand in for a whole lot of backstory,
as is the case in *How to Age Disgracefully* by Claire Pooley,
with a different POV character, Art. In this moment, he
considers an item (a staircase in his house) and, alongside it,
his entire history:

> Art climbed the stairs. The staircase he'd crawled
> up as a baby, tobogganed down in a sleeping bag as a
> child, then bounded up with his first girlfriend as a
> teenager, shedding articles of clothing on the way, then
> quickly retrieving them so they wouldn't be spotted by
> his mother. The staircase he could still picture his
> young wife climbing, with a mound of washing under
> one arm and a baby on her hip. Recently, climbing
> these stairs felt like ascending a small mountain.
> Today, more than ever.[ii]

Readers get an entire life in one passage, as well as the
protagonist's wide-ranging emotions about what's happened
to him.

On the other end of the spectrum, you can fill in context for a
specific facet of a character's backstory. In the case of the
psychological thriller *We Used to Live Here* by Marcus Kliewer,
we get Eve's relationship to religion. This notion does play
into the current plot, but not in a big way, so an entire
unpacking of her shifting faith would be overkill. Instead, we
get a cursory summary and can move on:

> Raised in a religious household, [Eve] never really had a problem with prayer. However, it had been nearly a decade since she'd said grace before a meal. *A whole decade?* Despite all the years gone by, the remnants of religion had clung to her like a strange aftertaste. Technically, Eve had stopped believing at seventeen years old, but her faith limped on well into her twenties, like staying in an obviously doomed marriage because, hey, maybe things will turn around eventually.[iii]

Notice how many of these excerpts do double duty. Through the image chosen to encapsulate Eve's loss of her own faith (a doomed marriage), and the notion that she'll stick with something long after she knows it's unhealthy or unhelpful, readers get the sense that she's not one to easily advocate for herself. And in this story, she doesn't, as she lets strangers into her house because she can't stand up for her own needs. As a result, Eve ends up in a psychological nightmare.

We also sometimes have to summarize a huge event that's going to impact everything else in the plot. This is the case in *The Fox Wife* by Yangsze Choo, as Snow connects her current desire for justice and revenge to what spawned it—her child's murder. We get a short snapshot of her consumed by grief, then transition to what she plans to do about it:

> The ache in my chest would never go away; a hollow, bloody darkness that had swallowed me for the last two years. Grass had grown on my child's grave in the far north. I'd lain on top of it every night for months, in vain hopes of keeping her warm. It was so cold, and she so small, lost to me forever. Burying my face in the dry clods of earth, I thought I'd die of grief and fury. But unlike the dead, living creatures recover. I clung to my vengeance grimly, that thin vein

of blood that pulsed and kept me alive. The man
who'd commissioned her death was a Manchurian
photographer named Bektu Nikan.[iv]

How much data do readers really need in order to *get it*? The loss of a child is an unbearably traumatic origin story (which we'll also touch upon in a bit when we talk about wound and need). It can be debilitating or galvanizing, and sometimes both. (It's also a favorite "dramatic backstory" element in storytelling, though some of us have, unfortunately, experienced this ourselves and have thoughts and feelings about it being used as easy shorthand for "the worst thing anyone can think of to happen to a person.")[3]

In the above sample, Snow recounts lying on her daughter's grave "in vain hopes of keeping her warm" and "burying [her] face in the dry clods of earth." Between these two images, readers will understand the emotional brunt of the trauma. Sure, the author could've gone on and on, but at some point, the ROI[4] decreases, and you run the risk of verging into melodrama and purple prose. The event almost speaks for itself in the sheer horror of it, so perhaps less is more.

What's interesting here is how Snow then transitions from the wound to the need—revenge. This is a very important use of backstory. Don't just include the information because you came up with it and feel like you need to get all that data across on the page. (You don't. With backstory, you need to be especially selective about what you ultimately include.) The above information is necessary because it directly influences

3. If you're curious, you can read more about my first daughter here:
https://kidlit.com/nora-pepper
4. Return on investment (of imagination, word count, narrative, etc.)

the choices this character makes, her objectives, and her deeper needs in the present.

Here's another example, from the thriller, *Everyone Who Can Forgive Me Is Dead* by Jenny Hollander, which also happens to leverage a dead child (I swear, I don't go out looking for these on purpose, they really are *that* common):

> My parents. They're in those photos, too. Even worse than Adam's smile are their hopeful, happy faces. There are tubes snaking out of their son, but they still look more joyful than I've ever seen them. So much younger, too, even though Adam died just a year before I was born. My mum and dad never once said it was up to me to make them proud, to live a spectacular life because Adam didn't get to, but seeing those pictures, day in and day out, it shamed me. I thought, *I can't keep letting them down.*[v]

This excerpt does a lot of heavy lifting. It uses the somewhat cliché mechanism of looking at family photos to present backstory. (If you do the same, know this is a very popular approach, as are therapy sessions.) We don't just learn about Adam here, but the effect his death had on Charlie's parents. They're no longer joyful, and that's a data point readers will want, as they only have the benefit of meeting them in this diminished state.

Most importantly, however, this translates into the character's self-imposed marching orders. Adam didn't get to live, so she must. She "can't keep letting them down." The parents have never said this outright, but with the backstory expressed here, the protagonist has made meaning from the past and allowed it to inform her present and potential future.

A more neutral backstory dump is used in *Home Is Where the*

Bodies Are by Jeneva Rose to summarize why Beth, one of the POV characters, decides to keep a secret from Susan:

> Lucas moved away after high school, and his father died in a hunting accident shortly thereafter. Emma's mother, Susan, still lives in the house across the street. Her health has been declining for years. I guess it's hard to stay healthy when you have a broken heart. Mom was close with Susan, and I think knowing what Mom kept from her all these years would kill her. So maybe the truth would do more harm than good at this point.[vi]

In this specific story, the family across the street ends up mattering to the present narrative. If these people didn't really play an active role, I would recommend not developing them in any kind of detail. But this is woven in early on so readers know their names and basic bios and are prepared to see whether these planted seeds end up germinating.

Sometimes the traumatic backstory that's summarized is a single event. Sometimes, it's an entire life story in several paragraphs. The below excerpt, from *A Reason to See You Again* by Jami Attenberg, encapsulates a life *and* tells about the father character using adjectives. It's the kind of "bad telling" the "show, don't tell" advice *and* this guide warn you about, but notice how the author uses it to paint a complete picture in only 73 words:

> He was daydreamy and faint and beautiful; their thin, pale Papa, who had been released from the camps barely a teenager, starved, starving, and made his way to American to exist as a hero in their eyes. The girls could not even imagine being as hungry as he had been. All of them wondered, marveled at his presence.

He knew how to hold a room—even if it was simply
by being alive.[vii]

We see the dad described, but we also see the joint POV of his
daughters, Shelly and Nancy ("the girls"), as they observe
him. The impressions we're given are filtered through their
empathy and admiration. While this example tells about
Papa, it also shows—in a much more subtle way—the love
these characters have for him. It's doing multiple things at
once, which elevates this excerpt from pure "bad telling."

That's a pro tip right there: If you use telling about backstory
or another character to show a POV protagonist interpreting
themselves, you can draw a direct line to the main character's
sense of self and identity. Then the telling (even if it's "about"
something else, at face value) serves to characterize your
protagonist more deeply.

The below is another example from *Trust* by Hernan Diaz.
This time it's about a complicated relationship between a
different POV character, Helen, and her father, who wanted to
mold her into his image. In fact, she's the complimentary
partner who ends up marrying the previous excerpt's POV,
Benjamin. Here's summary backstory of how she grew up
under his critical eye and how it impacted her:

Helen soon came to realize that in addition to
being her father's pupil she had become his object of
study. He seemed interested in the concrete results of
his teachings and tracked how they shaped his
daughter's mind and morals. When he examined her,
Helen often thought someone else was peering out
from behind his eyes. It was only in hindsight that she
saw that all this prying had driven her to create a
quiet, unassuming character, a role she performed with
flawless consistency around her parents and their

friends—inconspicuously polite, never speaking if it
could be helped, responding with nods and
monosyllables whenever possible, always looking
away from people's eyes, avoiding the company of
adults at all costs. That she never shed this persona
made her wonder, later in life, if that was not who she
had truly been all along or if, rather, over the years, her
spirit had shaped itself after the mask.[viii]

Not only do we get a download of Helen's early years, but
this sample imparts a sense of how these elements directly
impacted who she became in adulthood. This also presents
how she thinks about herself, which is, in and of itself,
illuminating. She's able to recognize she has "shaped [herself]
after the mask," which is rather astute analysis.

Our next example comes from the thriller *Look in the Mirror*
by Catherine Steadman. The character, Maria, was a migrant
and made a difficult journey to America with her family.
This is a traumatic backstory, and it plants the idea early on
that Maria is a protagonist with the grit and will to survive.
Since this is a suspense novel, that characteristic will be
directly tested (and we'll see that moment excerpted in
Chapter 8):

She feels a twinge of her past awakening inside
her. Her trauma—as always, buried just as far down as
she can stuff it—twitching back to life. Her very own
Frankenstein's monster, a shadow self, made up of off-
cuts, bits of memory and faded scares and half-
remembered images. The journey she made as a child
—the hunger, the thirst, the deep yawn of both inside
her, deeper than the cold, or the heat, or the fear, and
the dread of the adults around her disappearing,
dropping away, the memory of only the three of them
surviving. The three of them, alone, made it through

with the forest dirt and the shiver of what it took to
do so.[ix]

As you can see here, the author doesn't shy away from calling
the backstory outright "trauma" and labeling it directly.
Notice how we also, as with the *Trust* example, above, see
Maria manipulating her relationship to her past and
"[burying it] just as far down as she can stuff it." By seeing
how she interfaces with her memories, we learn about who
she is and her approach to life. This is the strange alchemy of
both telling the information and showing (via interiority) how
it's forged into who the protagonist is today. Readers get a lot
to interpret: Maria's overall attitude and how she approaches
the world around her. *That* part is transmuted without
outright explanation.

But not all backstory is tragic, harrowing, or inserted into a
story to prove a point. It can also be funny or galvanizing.
Which backstory you select for your characters and how you
present it will depend on the overall tone and character voice
you're going for.

Our last example in this section comes from a thriller as well,
but it's a darkly comedic one: *All the Other Mothers Hate Me* by
Sarah Harman. In this scene, the protagonist, Florence, a self-
proclaimed hot mess, is attending a bridal brunch for her
perfect (by comparison) sister, Brooke. The latter character
has done everything "right" and is reaping the rewards.
Here's how Florence expresses how Brooke has elevated
herself from their humble, messy roots. Readers can also
interpret Florence's envy about this magic trick:

> Brooke spent the next eight and a half years
> patiently waiting for Julian to propose. I told her it
> would never happen; Julian's family were the kind

with their name on a plinth outside the National Theatre, and Brooke was Florida trash, albeit trash with a carefully constructed accent. But it turns out Brooke was a lot better at marketing than I gave her credit for. At her engagement party, I'd overheard her telling one of Julian's great-aunts that our father had worked "in transportation" and our mother had been "a champion of Southern cuisine." I nearly choked on my canape. I suppose it's easy to whitewash the dead; they don't come back to haunt you with inconvenient truths. I, on the other hand, was a grenade waiting to explode all over her carefully sanitized version of our past.[x]

The truth is, their dad was a trucker and their mom, a Denny's waitress. But look how Brooke reframes the facts. What's told here is *about* Brooke, at face value, but as Florence talks about it, readers can dig deeper and interpret whether she feels she fits into this "sanitized version of [their] past." The information that's told is, once again, in conversation with the protagonist's identity.

Backstory is simply data. You have to select what makes the most sense for your character and narrative. From there, how a POV character interfaces with that data, relates to it, feels it has affected them, and presents it to readers and other characters is the marrow which makes it come alive.

How the backstory lives on in the present moment is expressed in the storytelling concept of character worldview, which we'll talk about next.

Worldview (Showing and Telling)

I invoked a favorite William Faulkner quote in *Writing Interiority*, and I'll reproduce it here:

"The past is never dead. It's not even past."

I take this to mean the past is active in a person's—and character's—present life. Of course, not every element of backstory is currently relevant. Not even in a memoir, where the past *is* a big part of the narrative. Because even in memoir, we must be selective about what we choose to include and the meaning we make from it. It's very rare in today's contemporary memoir market to write a true "cradle to the present moment" autobiography. Memoirs are built around tight focal topics and themes, and the events a writer chooses to narrate or tell about are ideally filtered through this lens.

In fiction, you might develop a lot of information about the character, but then you need to be similarly choosy about what you use and how it'll shape a reader's impression of your protagonist. The actual facts of the past, discussed above, can be put on the page. But they also come alive in other ways, including a protagonist's attitude and approach to life.

The worldview you include matters. And how you present it —and when—is a storytelling choice. Sometimes, a character will flat-out tell readers what they believe. Here's a basic example from *Happiness Falls* by Angie Kim, as Mia shares her perspective:

> Hope is dangerous that way; it leads you to confuse what's possible with what's not.[xi]

Mia doesn't want to hope because she thinks it's "dangerous." She probably doesn't trust that good things will happen in the future because they haven't panned out in the past. This colors her attitude and makes her wary of getting emotionally invested. Readers might be able to relate and understand where she's coming from because they understand both the conditions that created this belief system and the current plot that reinforces it. This is a blanket statement which reflects many elements of Mia's life and sense of self.

Other times, telling helps a writer weave a character's worldview directly with backstory summary. The following is from the upmarket thriller *The Quiet Tenant* by Clémence Michallon and explores a similar pessimistic outlook:

> Your childhood ends with the hope pretty much intact. Then, the teenage years begin, and the journey gets rockier. Your brother takes the pills. A first time, a second time. You learn to feel sad. You learn to occupy the hole in your parents' heart, the one that yearns for a golden child. You turn fifteen. You are ready for someone to see who you really are. You are ready for someone to love the true you.[xii]

This is a fantastic example because we get a tight summary of Rachel's upbringing from childhood to her teenage years. Notice she's using second-person direct address (the "you") in a bid to not only tell her story but pull readers right into it, breaking the fourth wall and basically forcing relatability. I may not have had a brother who took pills. I may not have had to "occupy the hole in [my] parents' heart," but the in-your-face nature of these statements is written to stoke empathy. What's interesting about this passage is how it not only connects the character's backstory and wound to their worldview, but, more importantly, to their need: to be seen for who she is. And that's a universal theme.

Here's another excerpt, this time, from *We Used to Live Here* by

Marcus Kliewer, which we first referenced earlier in this chapter:

> All seemed calm. Calm and quiet—both things that only served to heighten Eve's anxiety. When things felt right, it only meant there was so much more that could go wrong.[xiii]

This worldview is relevant to the current story because Eve is anxious and doesn't trust the things that "[feel] right" to *be* right. And, when it comes to the plot, she's, unfortunately, going to see her beliefs realized.

Sometimes, worldviews and belief systems are more specific to a plot in general, as we'll see in the following sample, from the romantic comedy *Guy's Girl* by Emma Noyes:

> Here's the thing about being a straight woman in a friend group of all straight men: there will inevitably be a complication. Either you'll fall for one of them, or one of them will fall for you. Sometimes it's mutual. In most cases, it isn't. And in the worst situation of all, one of them will chase you. He'll chase you hard, despite your repeated insistence that it's a terrible idea. He'll chase you until you give in. Until you fall for him.
> Then he'll break your heart as hard as he possibly can.[xiv]

From the title of the book, you easily get the sense that this is *the* premise. The story will explore what it's like to be a "guy's girl." The above "hypothetical" explanation is also exactly what ends up happening—at least in the initial conflict. While we're told Ginny's attitude, we are also primed to expect certain romantic tensions, which the book delivers.

In the following excerpt, from the thriller *The Hunter's Daughter* by Nicola Solvinic, Anna talks about growing up as a serial killer's daughter. She spent time with her father in the woods and the world around her became magical in its own way. This novel has a slight speculative element, so the woods *are*, in fact, alive. As she tries to figure out what this mindset means for her in the current story and in her life beyond childhood, "nothing was as it seemed" is not only a worldview, but a theme:

> I'd rather sink into the woods with my dad, who told me stories of spirits who lived among the trees. He'd tell me that everything was alive and listening in the forest: stones, trees, and especially animals. Everything I saw was magic: crows mimicking human speech; mirages of puddles that vanished when I approached; sticks that turned into snakes when I tried to pick them up. Nothing was as it seemed, but I accepted this, the brutality and the wonder of it.[xv]

Not only do we get a sense of Anna's relationship to her father, but to the entire natural world around her. This is telling about her perception of life. It also grounds readers in her foundation—the frame through which she experiences the present story. Yes, this is a simple statement, but it accomplishes multiple characterizing objectives at once.

In the following excerpt, from *Luster* by Raven Leilani, we go back to romantic relationships, but in an utterly fatalistic way. This character, Edie, has been chasing the wrong men throughout her life and this plays out in the present action when she has an affair with an older, married man and ends up pregnant. Here's how she applies her hard-won worldview to her situation as she makes a costume for Comic-Con and considers what might be going on inside her body:

>   I think of all the gods I have made out of feeble
> men. I go to my room and get stuck in a Wikipedia
> hole about religion on Tatooine. I finish my costume
> and sit in the dark in my metal bikini, and in the
> morning I stumble to the bathroom and take the
> pregnancy test. I am inclined to pray, but on principle,
> I don't. God is not for women. He is for the fruit. He
> makes you want and he makes you wicked, and while
> you sleep, he plants a seed in your womb that will be
> born just to die.[xvi]

It's suggested here that she will terminate the pregnancy
("born just to die"). What's even more painful is her idea that
"God is not for women" and that Edie has spent her youth
chasing "gods [she has made] out of feeble men." But what's
underlying this outright telling is what readers must
interpret: Maybe she wishes this wasn't true. These
statements suggest a deeper underlying need. What if she
could find a man to treat her well? What if she could turn her
soul over to a God who *is* listening to her?

With every statement of worldview, you have the opportunity
to implant something deeper: the wish beneath the opinion,
what the character believes *is*, and what they also wish
could be.

While the above example showcases powerlessness, a
character's worldview can also be leveraged into power, or at
least a coping strategy. In the following excerpt, from *Blue
Sisters* by Coco Mellors, Lucky spells out her perspective and
how she uses it to her advantage, even if she has to pretend
she's someone other than her true self:

>   Besides, as a model, Lucky was used to people
> taking pleasure in proving she was an idiot. It was a
> kind of protection against inadequacy, she assumed; if

she was pretty but dumb, they could still feel superior, even a little righteous, finding, in their own lack of marketable beauty, a confirmation of their higher intelligence. But if the two weren't causal? If it was possible to be both professionally attractive and smart? Then their own average looks served no purpose other than to disappoint, with Lucky acting as the hapless reminder. She'd found, in general, it was easier to keep her mouth shut and let people think whatever comforting thoughts they wanted about her. People seemed to hate her less that way.[xvii]

Here, Lucky boldly tells readers that she's both beautiful *and* smart, and that this notion is threatening to other people. She considers herself a mirror for their inadequacies and insecurities. As a result, Lucky makes her way through the world by letting characters around her decide who she is, because it's easier for *her* if she keeps her mouth shut and confirms whatever beliefs they have. She's an operator, and she's figured out a way to forge ahead, even if it's at the expense of being truly seen.

Our last excerpt presents an empowering worldview that also suggests who a character is and how she will move through the world. It comes from the sapphic vampire thriller, *Bury Our Bones in the Midnight Soil* by V.E. Schwab. In it, we meet María, who is born in a time and place that would rather not empower its women—Spain in the 1500s. She is expected to marry well, serve her husband, and glorify her family. But she doesn't want to do any of that shit:

> But María had known, all her life, that she is not meant for common paths, for humble houses and modest men. If she must walk a woman's road, then it will take her somewhere new.[xviii]

What María believes about herself is profoundly baked into who she is—and summarized succinctly in the above mission statement. The image of the "road" she walks follows her throughout the story. Moreover, this driving desire to make something new of herself, something better, something "uncommon," touches off literal centuries of empowerment bloodshed.[5]

This segues us nicely into the idea of telling about wound and need, which are foundational characterizing elements you can use to really anchor your protagonists as real, fully realized people who drive your story forward, as well as the notion of inner struggle.

---

5. Spoiler alert: Her road leads María to become a vampire.

6

WOUND, NEED, AND INNER STRUGGLE

Now we're getting into the real meat of it. Once you establish a character's sense of self, superficial objective and motivation, and their underlying backstory and worldview, you're ready to play several psychological layers below the surface. I've been referencing these ideas throughout, so they won't be completely unfamiliar, but let's kick off with a more comprehensive study of wound and need.

Wound and Need (Mostly Telling)

One of your jobs as a fiction or memoir writer is to present a character (or a curated version of yourself, in the case of memoir) who's proactively in pursuit of an objective, with strong emotional and intellectual logic undergirding it, otherwise known as their motivation.

Once we develop a deeper sense of the character's self and backstory, you can start to tease out the wound and need that might be driving them to act (often, in pursuit of self-actualization, but also sometimes against their own best interests).

Conventional storytelling wisdom says there should be something in your character's backstory (whether episodic and acute or long-running and chronic) that creates a need within them. If it's the car accident example from the previous chapter, they might be haunted by the impossible need to have their family back together. Since this cannot happen in their present life because their sibling died, they might instead fill this need by reconnecting with their parents after a period of estrangement or creating their own family as a way of healing their wound.

If it's emotional neglect, they might need to be seen and appreciated for who they are. If that's not possible within their family or origin, the character might become especially interested in finding a loving romantic partner or getting professional approval from their mentor—both of which would bolster their feelings of worth and value. They might not realize what they're doing or why at first, but this understanding usually dawns on them (and readers) by the end.

Often, the wound is the origin story for the need, and the need is what will help the character break through to the next level in their evolution. Now, it's perhaps unrealistic that a character will go through a plot and feel their need is met entirely, meaning they will never crave anything on a deeper level, and never experience a void at their center again.

It's also unreasonable to think that a character will never develop another need which will also require the same soul-searching and fulfillment-finding process. Finally, it'd be silly to imagine that a character will be all "fixed" and will never experience tension or conflict once their need is met, or that they'd never backslide into needing more affirmation or validation.

But for the purposes of story structure, even if other wounds and needs crop up down the line, the met need requires a re-up, and/or the character still feels like there's something missing in their lives, the most pressing and emotionally resonant need is still met by the end of the current plot, and the wound seems—if not *healed*—more manageable.

While we can use flashback to convey the moment a wound takes root, telling and interiority are generally used to suggest the underlying need, especially if the character is only themself becoming aware of it and its genesis.

Much like we often use telling to explore objective and motivation, it's entirely appropriate to tell about need. The only difference is that need often functions below the surface, so its expression tends to be less explicit. This is where readers will need to put on their detective hats and dig between the lines, but that's perfect for wound and need, as they are buried under the protagonist's surface, too, so audiences (and the characters themselves) expect to do more exploring.

Here are some examples from the shelves. Our first comes in scene form, between Grace, the protagonist of the upmarket novel, *Amazing Grace Adams* by Fran Littlewood, and her daughter, Lotte. This conversation happens later in the story, as Grace is confronting the unvarnished truth that she has previously gone away to deal with her mental health struggles. It is, in fact, a reveal to readers and the protagonist that a) Grace has been trying to run away from the impact this has had on her family, and b) that Lotte is aware of what happened and needs to talk about it. Lotte is acting out at school, racking up demerits, and Grace tries to play the responsible adult and mother her. What she gets in return is a slap in the face:

> "What's with the absences?" Lotte's voice is a

harmonic. "You're asking *me* that? What about your big *absence*, huh?" She flicks her index fingers like knives, putting air quotes around the word. "You left us for—how long was it, Mum? Remind me. I'd have to go some to match it, wouldn't I? We never talk about that, do we?" She pauses, and when she speaks again it's as though she's talking to herself. "We never ever did."

Grace stands, stunned, as her daughter pushes herself off the stairs, disappears down the landing. And as the bedroom door bangs shut she sinks to the floor where she's standing. It's as though the oxygen has been sucked from the hallway. She feels dizzy. What has just happened. Grace is struggling to understand. Her mind is slipping and sliding, trying to reconcile what she knows with what she thought she knew. She can't believe what Lotte has just said to her, because her daughter is right: they have never discussed the time she left, not ever. It's so long ago now and Grace has allowed herself to believe that maybe—*maybe*—Lotte had forgotten.[i]

There are a lot of layers to unpack here. First up is the revelation that Lotte is not only aware of Grace's absence (of course she is, and it was delusional for Grace to think she somehow glossed over it, just because it might've been easier). Second, that the wound is still very much festering. From the telling that "Grace stands, stunned" and "Grace is struggling to understand," readers are left to extrapolate Grace's objective: for this to just go away.

It'd be neater and nicer if Grace had taken the time she needed for herself without leaving a big, ugly mark on her family. On some level, she wants this to be the truth because she feels guilty. But this isn't the case. Once the wound is out in the open, Grace must deal with it. Not only for herself—to metabolize her own shame—but for her daughter. What Grace might *want* is for this to blow over. What she actually *needs* is to heal—but for real this time.

Notice that we also have some physical clichés in her response ("She feels dizzy") but the author quickly pushes into interiority to support the bodily reaction.

The next two excerpts come from *The Wedding People* by Alison Espach, and they explore Phoebe's character development. Remember, she showed up to an exclusive hotel to die by suicide, then got wrapped up in the human drama and comedy of an unfolding destination wedding. Here's how she unpacks what her actual need is, and it's *not* to drown herself in the ocean:

> Her therapist was right. She won't kill herself. She is not the type. She has always known this about herself but somehow forgot. Somehow, everything felt so dark back at home, and only now that she is here can Phoebe look back and see just how dark … To be stuck inside her house was to be stuck inside herself and all the choices she made over the years.[ii]

This passage explores "just how dark" she got in her own head after her husband left her for another woman. As a result, she decided to end things because she couldn't see another way out of it after being "stuck inside herself and all the choices she made over the years." However, once she arrives and gets a taste of another life and more possibilities, she is able to pull out of her nosedive. What she initially *wanted* was to stop the pain, but what she *needs* is to heal her wound and figure out just what living might look like now that her former existence has fallen apart.

We saw an excerpt of Phoebe's relationship to books and stories in Chapter 2. As she moves on to her own next chapter, this is how she feels about them now, and it's a very clear explanation of her need's evolution:

> She is so good at predicting what will happen in books, so bad at predicting what will happen in life. That is why she has always preferred books—because to be alive is much harder. To be alive, she must leave this hotel, despite the uncertainty of everything.[iii]

This passage hits as she's once again leaving her situation, but this time, it's the new life she discovered for herself at the hotel. And while "to be alive is much harder" than anything she can find in her beloved literature, she has chosen to rise up and meet life on its own terms. It's not going to be predictable—and in a very real way, she *needs* things to be clear and straightforward—but Phoebe has decided to soldier on regardless instead of putting an end to the uncertainty by taking herself out of the narrative.

As you can see, needs are often basic and deal with the most foundational elements of character and theme. Here's an example of a childhood wound manifesting as an adult need from the Southern gothic horror novel *This Cursed House* by Del Sandeen, as the protagonist, Jemma, grapples with what it might mean to be accepted by Honorine, the family matriarch:

> She hated the small part of her, the hurt childlike part hiding its face behind little hands, that wanted exactly that, wanted nothing more than to have Honorine accept her as one of her own, introduce her as her granddaughter, look at her with love instead of indifference at best.[iv]

This is what I'd call an "objective versus need" situation. The character's stated desire is to be honored, loved, and accepted. That's what personhood is all about, isn't it? To be seen, to have someone reach out and say, "It's okay. No matter who or what you are, we want you for your essence." But readers must think beyond what's told and interpret what it means. Here, I'd go so far as to say that Jemma must figure out a way to love herself and give herself the acceptance she craves, or the wound and need will never be fulfilled. If she's waiting on other people to make her feel truly valued, she's likely going to be waiting a long time. Others are never going to give us what we fully need to give ourselves.

Of course, not all characters are going to be evolved enough to realize how their needs are driving their actions or to metabolize them enough to heal their wounds. One of my favorite antihero characters is June from *Yellowface* by R.F. Kuang. She's a struggling writer and steals a rival's manuscript because she believes she needs to be vindicated through traditional publishing, fame, and fortune. (Relatable?) Here, she expresses what's driving her:

> "I can't rely on my old work," I say, though I know I can't make her understand. "I need to write the next best thing. And then another. Otherwise the sales will whittle down, and people will stop reading my work, and everyone will forget about me." Saying this out loud makes me want to cry. I hadn't realized how much this terrified me: being unknown, being forgotten. I sniffle. "And then when I die, I won't have left any mark on the world. It'll be like I was never here at all."[v]

At face value, this is pure self-explanation through dialogue and supported by interiority. Showing would blur this naked fear, while telling gives it clarity and stakes. She *must* do this or (she believes) her life won't matter: "It'll be like I was never here at all." She clearly examines the terror of being

89

forgotten. But if we dig below the surface, we can see she's justifying her actions. June is building an unimpeachable case for herself and explaining away what she's done to soothe her own conscience. Of course, this *sounds* valid. Who wants to be irrelevant? Who wants all of their work and energy to be for *nothing*?

At the same time, the wound and need operating underneath are based in insecurity. She has previously tried to publish her *own* work and been unsuccessful. As a result, she feels deeply hurt by a world which doesn't seem to want her. The (warped, cracked, maybe slightly insane) solution? To cut out the parts publishing doesn't seem to want—her unique contributions—and replace them with a sure thing (a manuscript by a famous friend who met an untimely end). She believes that if she's able to put *something* out into the world and the establishment deems it worthwhile, then, by the Wounded Character Transitive Property, *she* will be worthwhile.

What's told is one thing, but the need that pulses below it must be unearthed by a careful reader and examined for its flawed logic. Engaged audiences will understand that she will never truly meet the need driving her to act because, at the end of the day, we all know the work isn't hers. Her newfound bestseller status is a shallow victory. June reveals she'll never truly feel secure because she knows, just as audiences do, that it's not really her *own* creativity winning accolades. And, even worse, she worries it'll go away at any minute and her deception will be discovered. By "meeting" this need the wrong way, she's only opening another wound.

Our last quote in this section comes from the literary novel *Same As It Ever Was* by Claire Lombardo, and it's a beautiful summary of a character realizing she's been chasing the wrong thing her entire life. We meet Julia at midlife, as she explains how she's spent years hoping to be perceived a certain way, only to learn this was a false need all along:

> She wishes now that she had spent all the years she worried about other people thinking she was weird actually *being* weird.[vi]

I love this from the bottom of my heart. One thing I've been telling writers for years now is to pursue their own *weird*. Depending on your goals, of course, you might get "too weird" for traditional publication, which is a rant in and of itself. But more often than not, the thing that makes your work truly *yours* is the unique, specific stuff you bring to it that only you can add. Yes, publishing is a tough industry where you feel you have to chase what the establishment, gatekeepers, and tastemakers want, just as June from *Yellowface* does.

And yet you can sometimes lose yourself and your artistic and creative vision in the process. What if life and self-expression aren't about what other people think of you? What if it's about bringing your full, unvarnished, examined, and realized self to the page?

Needs are basic and come from a handful of foundational wounds we all tend to experience at one point or another: rejection, embarrassment, shame. If you, the writer, create characters who are better able to serve their own needs, there will be a whole lot of healing and self-actualization baked into the deepest and most profound levels of your stories, as well as into your own writing journey. But, of course, none of this is simple. It involves a huge load of inner struggle, which is what we'll talk about next.

Inner Struggle (Mostly Telling)

To tie together some of these subterranean character layers, we have the idea of inner struggle. It's the sum total of a character's flip-flopping, uncertainty, self-loathing, self-defeat, things they wish they could change about themselves, and anything else that makes them flawed, unreasonable, or messy.

Sometimes characters express blanket inner struggle (usually tied to their personality). They can also be in conflict with themselves episodically—for example, about an important decision they must make, but which will involve downsides or stakes everywhere they look.

Interiority and telling are great tools for rendering inner struggle on the page. In fact, I made this concept one of interiority's five key pillars, along with thoughts, feelings, reactions, and expectations. Sometimes, there's no better way to explore a complex, oblique, or contradictory issue like this one than to be explicit. When the character is in crisis, let readers know. When it comes to conflict below the surface, this is where "show, don't tell" completely breaks down, and you potentially leave a lot of richness and character development on the table.

There's a big difference between a woman standing on a bridge and looking out at the view, and one who's saying her final goodbyes to the world and everyone she loves in her head because she's about to jump. But externally—the domain of showing—the woman looks the same in both scenarios (unless she's pacing or crying in the latter circumstance, of course).

It's the internal component—the telling about her inner struggle—that's going to add an entirely different layer to what the eyes can see and what the body can show or suggest. That's obviously a dramatic example,[1] but it illustrates the limitations and one-dimensionality of showing while reminding us of the richness we can leave unexplored if we don't add some telling.

Of course, there's still an art to expressing this kind of nuanced information well and still giving readers detective work to do, and that's what I'll demonstrate in the examples which follow.

Since we were recently spelunking around in worldview, let's start with an excerpt from *When Women Were Dragons* by Kelly Barnhill, as Alex chafes against the rules of her household. Her aunt has become a dragon, leaving Alex's family to raise her niece, Beatrice, as her sister. This is wearing on her, as is the entire family ethos of keeping secrets and maintaining appearances:

> What could I say? I wanted to tell Beatrice the truth, but I didn't know where to begin. Maybe start with the fact that my mother forced me to lie and lie and lie, and how we built our family on that lie, and eventually most believed in that lie. Beatrice was my sister. I had no aunt. We did not speak of dragons. My mother was gone, but her rules were *still here*. And, frankly, it felt comfortable to keep living with her rules. And safe.[vii]

The crux of Alex's inner struggle with this domestic culture and larger story world is summarized by "how we built our family on that lie." Even though Alex's mother has since died, "her rules were *still there*." And while Alex feels "comfortable

---

1. No disrespect is meant to those who struggle with suicidal ideation by invoking this image to prove a writing craft point. I've been on that bridge myself a few times, figuratively, if not literally.

to keep living her rules," and maybe even "safe," she is erupting beneath the surface to stop lying and live the truth she knows. When the external situation doesn't match a character's inner life, sense of self, or notion of identity, this is the marrow of inner struggle.

A similar example comes from the literary novel *Shred Sisters* by Betsy Lerner, as Amy wrestles with her sister, Ollie's, drug use and breakdown:

> Also terrifying was how quickly we resumed our routines and roles. Mom returned to her bridge and tennis games, Dad to work and golf, though he was away a lot more now. Mom complained about his absences, but her protests were hollow: each of us was comfortably siloed. In the beginning, I couldn't grasp how it was going to work. Were we never going to talk about Ollie? Sometimes I guiltily hoped she would die; our grief would have an end point.[viii]

This character must hold two truths at once: She wants and needs her family to be "okay" (whatever that means) on the surface, and she also wants everyone to be *truly* whole and healed. However, none of this can happen while Ollie is in her addiction and acting out. Living with an addict is incredibly painful. On the one hand, there's love for the person. On the other, there's endless trauma without any identifiable end, which means it's sometimes easier to wish for that person to finally die so they stop wreaking havoc and uncertainty. If Ollie dies, at least Amy will be able to start grieving, and the family might finally face all of their issues head-on.

But Amy doesn't want Ollie to die, per se. She simply wants the pain to end. What she really needs, deep down, I'd wager to guess, is for Ollie to heal so everyone can enjoy a family that isn't "siloed." But that's denial and magical thinking.

While Amy tells us death might be easier, this is also juicy inner struggle played out on the page. What she needs is something she can't have, and that's why it hurts.

Our next excerpt comes from the literary novel *Human Blues* by Elisa Albert. The protagonist, Aviva, has clear voice and self-knowledge, but she keeps dashing herself against an obstacle: She can't get pregnant. Infertility is one of those life experiences that has the capacity to truly break a person who wants to become a parent. A baby is the endgame, but the underlying desire is often deeper. Someone struggling with infertility is standing on the precipice of a big "What if?" Not everyone is driven to procreate, but for those who are, this turns into the ultimate quest. And the stakes are high. Not becoming a parent, for a person who may have wanted to for as long as they've been aware of the concept, is a deep fear. And if trying naturally or using fertility treatments isn't successful, there's a horrible (to them) outcome: They may never get to experience something they deeply crave. It's an either/or. You either have a baby, or you don't. You either become a parent and unlock an entire lifetime of experiences, or you don't. There's also a lot of body identity and personhood wrapped into it. Are you not "good enough" to become a parent? Is your body (or your partner's body) failing you? With something so personal, it's tough not to take it personally.[2] So there's a lot of inner struggle involved. Here's the excerpt:

> She'd been easygoing about the whole thing for a

2. Ask this three-time IVF veteran how I know all about it! (Happily, I have three living children now, but my husband and I spent years deeply afraid it'd never happen.) And for those who always point out the fact that there are many adoptable and deserving children in the world, that's fine and good. But this ignores the desire some people have for biological children. While it's a valid and worthwhile route to family-building, it can be an unhelpful or painful suggestion to someone struggling with infertility.

long time: Whatever happened, happened. It would happen! Of course it would. It would happen. No need to stress. No need to freak out. The important thing was not to freak out—everyone knew that. She was (relatively) happy, she was (relatively) healthy, she was in the green half of her thirties, she was in a lovely relationship, and tiiiii-i-i-iiiime was on her side, yes, it was. But at some point—a year of negatives? Two? Going on three—she'd gotten real quiet. Confused. Scared. Mad. Sad. She'd gritted her teeth, dug in her heels, and tried to find a way to inhabit the situation with a modicum of dignity. She read all the books, listened to all the podcasts. She changed her diet, her perspective, her expectations. She "made space." She "summoned the spirits." She "gathered the bones."

And still: nothing. Nothing. Nothing! Negative pee stick upon negative pee stick upon negative pee stick. Cycle after cycle after cycle. And by now she was straight-up furious. Incensed. What the actual *fuck*. Now she was outright begging. Come the fuck *on*. *Please*! Seriously. There was no dignity in it now. Now she was foaming at the mouth. Now she was gnashing her teeth and muttering to herself. Now she was half-insane with the injustice of it. Now any pregnancy anywhere near her orbit felt like a low branch to the eye.[ix]

First of all, I love the voice here, perhaps because I can deeply relate. But spelled out this way, I think most people will be able to at least see where Aviva is coming from, even if they don't have the same drive to have a baby. What I really like about this statement of inner struggle is how Aviva reflects it back and subsumes it at the level of identity. She goes from thinking of herself as "easygoing about the whole thing for a long time" to seeing herself as lacking "dignity" and "half-insane." The surface-level issue at hand is achieving a pregnancy, but what's roiling underneath is deep conflict with the self.

Our final inner struggle example comes from *The Remarkable Journey of Coyote Sunrise* by Dan Gemeinhart, a middle grade novel about a girl, Coyote, who lives with her dad, Rodeo, in a van. This is obviously a quirky set-up, but it's hiding a terrible wound: the mother and sisters died in a car crash, so Dad packed Coyote up and took off on a journey across the country. But Coyote is slowly realizing that they can't outrun their grief. When they pick up a hitchhiker, Salvador, and he turns a mirror on their unconventional life, Coyote is forced to grapple with her situation:

> "It works for us," I said.
>
> "Does it?" he asked. "I mean, maybe it works for *him*. But does it work for you ... *Coyote*?"
>
> He said my name the way people do when they curl their fingers in the air like sarcastic quotation marks. He said my name like it was a joke, like a punch line, like an elbow to the ribs.
>
> My throat hurt. My stomach churned.
>
> I am not a mess. I am not a joke. I am not fragile. I am not broken.
>
> I stood up, bent down, and picked up Ivan, a limp body and a weak *squeak* his only protest at being disturbed mid-nap.
>
> "I'm going to bed," I said to anyone who happened to be listening, and I walked back with my cat and I pulled the curtain to my room closed behind me and I slept just fine, thank you.[x]

This scene represents the beginning of Coyote's awakening to what she really needs. We also get a well-worn physical cliché here ("My stomach churned") but the author immediately supports it with interiority. As you can see from Coyote's reaction to Salvadore's prodding, she *wants* to convince herself she is "just fine, thank you." That's what's told at face value. But if we look again, we might see this is defensiveness talking. The suggestion is she's *not* fine, and, in fact, she ends up concocting a plan to go back home for the first time since the tragedy so she can confront the trauma head-on. While Coyote might be on the verge of breaking open and really tackling the source of her inner struggle, to heal her wound and meet her need for healing, she must also work on Rodeo, who's busy pretending *he's* "just fine, thank you," too, and that the whole vanlife adventure is a choice, rather than a grief reaction. The courage it'll take Coyote to fight for the truth is going to define her character development arc.

This brings us to the end of our exploration of telling as it applies to your POV protagonist and their myriad foundational elements. But there are other characters in most stories, like Rodeo, and they need to be examined through the lens of showing and telling, too.

SECONDARY CHARACTERS AND RELATIONSHIPS

"Show, don't tell" means you only have action and dialogue available to you when it comes to character depiction, as discussed in Chapter 3. And this is especially true with secondary characters where readers are shut out of POV access. It's all showing, baby!

Or is it?

Because your POV can also explain and interpret the rest of the cast. This adds a layer of telling. However, remember that *everything* a protagonist says and thinks is biased. Their experience is just one version of events. Especially in memoir. So if a character explains their sister or friend or nemesis, we're getting a slanted sense of the person in question, guaranteed. And reader impressions play a big role here, just as they do with the audience's take on your protagonist.

Think of the people you know in your life. There are going to be very few that you're truly neutral about. In fact, aggressively neutral people usually get a bad label: "That Chuck from accounting is so booooooring!" Keep this in mind. Even your normally level-headed protagonist might have polarized or exaggerated opinions about secondary characters.

Readers will have to take what the main character says about any secondary character and match it against their own interpretations, as we initially discussed in Chapter 2. And audiences are usually fantastic about keeping their wits about them and sniffing out bias. If they like a secondary character, while a protagonist obviously does *not*, this creates an interesting dynamic. However, if the reader's esteem tips too far in this direction—and they start to enjoy the so-called villain more than the hero—you could potentially lose their engagement.

Telling can be useful to summarize key data points about secondary characters, but those should then either be supported or contradicted by how those secondary characters talk, act, and treat the protagonist.

In a counterpoint to the above, keep in mind that characters can lie, and they will absolutely be pursuing their own needs and objectives in scene. So how a secondary character acts and what they say—our two most potent ways to evaluate them—can easily be manipulated for effect.

Maybe Chuck from accounting is boring at work because he just wants to clock in, get his projects done, and go home. The less he bothers with anyone, the faster he can return to his *real* passion, which is Victorian dollhouse restoration. When you get him on *that* topic, he's anything but dull. In fact, he might never shut up.

But if our POV protagonist only works with Chuck, readers are unlikely to be privy to this information. Our main character can turn on *Antiques Roadshow* on a fluke and catch Chuck in his element, or stumble upon his Etsy shop, but otherwise, Chuck isn't likely to reveal his true self.

If a secondary character hates or loves your protagonist, readers will see *that* side of them. For example, in Gloria Chao's[1] *The Ex-Girlfriend Murder Club*, a romantic comedy thriller, Tanner, the boyfriend, is *triple*-timing three women. But the Tanner readers meet through the protagonist's lovestruck perspective is definitely not who he ends up being. Then Tanner dies, and the wronged ex-girlfriends are obvious suspects.

Readers only meet Tanner alive for a few scenes, in which he's first a doting boyfriend, then a jerk caught in the act. We learn more about him as facts come out and the protagonist interfaces with other people who knew him. That novel is a great example of how many tools you have at your disposal when it comes to portraying a secondary character and shaping protagonist *and* reader perception.

I'm not saying you need to devote reams of paper to creating every secondary character's backstory, wound, need, and inner struggle, but if the members of your supporting cast behave consistently from interaction to interaction and character to character, they're too flat. They need dimension, and maybe some goals and ulterior motives.

However, if they're so complex and interesting that you're chomping at the bit to be released from the limitations of not giving them a POV, go into their heads, too, and write multiple perspectives. Just keep your POV sections or chapters separate so you avoid the cardinal sin of head-hopping (dipping into multiple characters' heads in one scene).

For now, consider devoting some attention to thinking about how each secondary character acts on the surface—to your

---

1. I did a great Thriving Writers podcast interview with her. You can find it here: https://www.thrivingwriterspodcast.com/episodes/gloria-chao

protagonist and others—and how you might reveal additional nuance with the tools at your disposal, which are primarily dialogue and action.

You can also use:

- Found materials—like Chuck's Etsy shop, or a journal or letter that a protagonist might stumble upon— which show a new side to a non-POV character;
- Recollections *about* the secondary character from someone who isn't the protagonist;
- Surprising news about what a secondary character is doing in the current plot—for example, they're gearing up to run for the protagonist's city council seat out of the blue, which is a total betrayal;
- Overheard conversations the POV isn't meant to eavesdrop on, where a secondary character drops their act; and
- The POV protagonist's reaction to the secondary character, including their interpretation of what might be going on beneath the surface, their motives, etc. (These impressions can be unreliable, but if the primary point-of-view character is making these judgments, readers are more or less going to take their opinions into consideration.)

Some of these information delivery mechanisms might seem like hokey plot conveniences, but there is a certain level of contrivance that most audiences will tolerate when it comes to establishing information about a non-POV character. These tricks for revealing information have been done before, so take some of the pressure off to reveal secondary character data in a way that's completely innovative. The idea doesn't have to be new, it just has to be well done and make sense for the story you're writing. As Dolly Parton says, "It takes a lot of time and money to look this cheap." What we see at face value often has intentional craft and story logic operating underneath. Someone on Goodreads might still call it a "plot hole" or a "contrivance," sending you to reevaluate every idea you've ever had over a double pour of wine, so do your best. And go ahead and tell, while you're at it.

The key question you should ask yourself is: How do my secondary characters reveal themselves in addition to what readers are told about them?

Here are some examples of showing and telling about secondary characters, so we can see these concepts in action.

From the Shelves

Our first example is a biased take from Ginny in *Guy's Girl* by Emma Noyes. She's the one who's friends with a tightly knit group of guys—but with an undercurrent of romantic feelings constantly swirling:

> There he is: Alex Finch, the fourth and final corner of their friend group. Sitting in a low armchair, aux cord plugged into his phone, guitar balanced on his lap. Finch is studying to become an orthopedic surgeon at NYU. He has close-cropped blond hair and a crooked smile. He's completely brilliant and also stupid, in the way that all brilliant men are also stupid.[i]

Alex Finch doesn't end up being Ginny's primary romantic interest, but this is a cute and funny introduction to someone from their group just the same. We immediately get the contrast of a playful and disheveled yet paradoxically ambitious young man. Then Ginny takes it an extra mile with the great (yet biased) line about him being "completely brilliant and also stupid," which adds fun voice and her own worldview. And Ginny would know, because the premise of the story is that she's literally a guy's girl, so she has a lot to say on the topic.

The following character portraits come from *The Wedding People* by Alison Espach, and, this time, we're meeting Lila and Gary—the "happy" couple who have gathered everyone at the hotel for their wedding. Except cracks are showing. Lila is attracted to the best man, and Gary is falling for … Phoebe, our narrator. She knows it's wrong, but she can't help hoping the bride and groom will see how badly suited they are for one another. Lila, especially, gets an ungenerous depiction. Phoebe likes her but isn't afraid to call out how fake she can be:

> The difference between Lila inside Phoebe's hotel room and Lila outside Phoebe's hotel room is becoming jarring to Phoebe. Phoebe has become used to Lila's honesty, the storming in, the sitting down, the immediate confession about whatever it was that was making her unhappy. It made Phoebe feel like a priest or a therapist. But out here, around these women, Lila is private. Guarded.[ii]

Lila may be the subject of this telling, but look at what we learn about Phoebe as she discusses someone else. She seems to like feeling needed and she appreciates Lila's honesty, even if she feels put-upon. Notice she says their relationship "made [her] feel like a priest or a therapist" rather than "like a friend." But if we dig even deeper into this assessment of Lila, we might see Phoebe judging her.

Beneath "Lila is private. Guarded," there's almost an undercurrent of "What's wrong with her?" and "Why can't she be herself around her friends?" and even "Which version of Lila is the *real* thing?" You should try to have your evaluation of secondary characters do double duty and fold back over to reveal something intended or unintended about your protagonist, too.

In the next excerpt, we see Phoebe take a shine to Gary, who is getting married for the second time after the tragic loss of his wife. Notice how she glows about him and how unafraid she is to find someone else's fiancé "incredibly sexy" in the run-up to his wedding. Phoebe did go to that hotel to try and die, so, arguably, she has few fucks to give about propriety and social mores, but notice the tonal contrast between her descriptions of Lila and the groom:

> There is something incredibly sexy to Phoebe about Gary's gray hairs ... She is drawn to the exhaustion of a lived life, to the man who has loved deeply and then lost suddenly and carries on. A man who has buried his wife and walked away and woke up to peel potatoes for dinner. A man who has lived through enough to appreciate the stones beneath his feet.[iii]

What's really interesting about this novel is how Lila and Gary have both public and private relationships with Phoebe. We see Gary and Lila interacting with one another in both public and private, too! Who are they when they're in front of their families, playing the happy couple? Who are they when they're hissing at one another behind closed doors? Phoebe is privy to all of these various versions, and this novel is a master class in how multi-faceted you can make your non-POV characters.

The next excerpt, from *Midnight Is the Darkest Hour* by Ashley Winstead, the Southern gothic thriller, features more open-ended telling about a secondary character:

Everett's a mechanic like his father. It turns out
that even if you hate your family, you still inherit from
them. But unlike his father, who planted his garage
here in Bottom Springs, Ever's an itinerant mechanic,
unable to commit to any town for more than a few
months at a time. I've never been able to get to the
bottom of his restlessness.[iv]

Though this is a first-person narrator reflecting on her closest
friend, you might remember Ruth's unique character voice
from Chapter 3, where she talked about herself in the third
person. Her tone sounds omniscient because of the summary
telling, but this passage layers in tone and social context, as
well as Ruth's own worldview ("even if you hate your family,
you still inherit from them").

Next up is another excerpt from *When Women Were Dragons*
by Kelly Barnhill. While the narrator, Alex, and her mother
"stay put," her aunt partakes in the dragoning:

The room grew suddenly hot. My aunt was big
and loud and *shiny*. Sometimes she laughed louder
than any man I knew. I found her thrilling, but
terrifying too. She had a way of occupying a room that
felt dangerous. She was heat and claw and intentional
velocity.[v]

This description by turns conveys the protagonist's
admiration, awe, and fear. There's also an undercurrent of
societal expectations and cultural worldviews here: "she
laughed louder than any man I knew" and "she had a way of
occupying a room that felt dangerous." Both refer to how the
aunt defied what it meant to be a woman in that time.

Our final secondary character description excerpt is another
masterclass, with amazing voice, to boot, so buckle in. It

comes from the literary novel *The Rabbit Hutch* by Tess Gunty and goes into a secondary character, Jack's, POV. Jack is a foster system teen and rough around the edges. He lives with a number of other characters, including the story's seventeen-year-old protagonist,[2] Blandine, in a group home. While we do inhabit Blandine's perspective in other sections, the following is an external evaluation of her:

> Blandine doesn't talk about the bad stuff that happened to her before she met us, but you can tell her bad stuff was fucking *bad*. Can tell by the way she scrubs her hands raw with the steel wool in the kitchen. By the giant religious books she lugs around. The bird nests and twigs and valley shit she collects. Animal bones. Sometimes, when she's not home, I snoop around her room, which smells like weed and roses. Glass bottles of spiky plants crowd the windowsills. Above her bed, she's taped depressing internet biographies of people no one's ever heard of. She keeps a lot of Venus fly traps.
>
> No one has it easy in the Vacca Vale system, but Blandine had it the worst, being so smart and female. People want things from the Blandines of the system, and I'm sure her brain didn't help. Thinking too much can zap you dead, and Blandine—she just shuts herself in rooms and thinks. Thinks and thinks and thinks herself into all kinds of doom, and by sundown she's afraid of the doorknob. She's the only one of us who

---

2. This novel is for adult readers for a number of reasons, and I want to take this moment to remind you that not every story with or about a child, tween, or teenage protagonist is a children's, middle grade, or young adult book, respectively. If you want to learn more about writing for those target audiences, please check out my other guides: *Writing Irresistible Picture Books: Insider Insights Into Crafting Compelling Modern Stories for Young Readers* and *Writing Irresistible Kidlit: The Ultimate Guide to Crafting Fiction for Young Adult and Middle Grade Readers*.

would've gone to college. Once, I found a letter in her bedroom from some guidance counselor—an email she must've printed out—pushing her to apply to the Ivy Leagues. The counselor said she had a real shot at admission. We have no idea why Blandine dropped out. She was a scholarship student at the only fancy high school in town. Only one more year to go. She never talked about it. If you ever mentioned any kind of school to her, she'd either lecture you about how fucked-up the American education system is or she'd bolt.[vi]

Jack's snarky observational voice makes the telling immersive and emotionally loaded. It's biased, rhythmic, and judgmental—in other words, alive. The details he notices (and which the author has intentionally chosen), like the Venus fly trap and the smell of "weed and roses" do a lot of heavy lifting. Nothing here is mentioned without purpose, even if Jack is describing all the seemingly random junk in a teen girl's room. The repetition isn't scenic—it's lyrical telling that reveals voice, Jack's perspective, Blandine's mannerisms, habits, secrets, and the story's emotional atmosphere all at once. It's very clear that Blandine is hiding her true self from those around her—she presents herself to readers differently when we're in her POV. Having this additional insight from someone who's observing her serves to complicate and deepen the reader's overall understanding of the protagonist, as well as giving us insight into Jack himself.

Let's pivot not just to secondary character descriptions, but to passages of telling (sometimes combined with showing and some dialogue) which attempt to encapsulate entire relationships. We're weaving together secondary character description, protagonist sense of self, backstory, and summary now!

Character Relationships

Our first example is another excerpt from *Shred Sisters* by
Betsy Lerner, where Amy talks about Ollie, her troubled sister
(whose death—though it was actually magical thinking with
an eye toward self-soothing—she wished for in Chapter 6):

> I know I could never enter my sister's world. She
> was daring and reckless. She slept naked, while I wore
> pajamas over underpants and undershirts. She
> scooped out avocados with two fingers and plunged
> the meat into her mouth. Without hesitation, Ollie
> would dive off a cliff into a reservoir, jump on a horse
> and canter into the woods. Ollie was *that* girl. First in,
> last out. What no one yet understood was that Ollie
> had no brakes.[vii]

This telling uses contrasts to set up the protagonist and Ollie
as foils. We also get some examples of Ollie's personality, then
ominous future forecasting ("what no one yet understood").
The latter approach is tricky because it can pull readers out of
the fictive dream and remind them that they're reading a
story and the author and protagonist already know the
ending. Here, we widen the narrative distance a little bit
because Amy seems to have already lived this narrative. She's
reflecting on a past version of herself, but she knows what
ends up happening with Ollie. This can be jarring in first-
person POV (and theoretically impossible in first-person
present tense), as readers like to feel immersed. If a character
hints that they already know what's coming, it only
emphasizes the inherent contrivance of storytelling. But
notice how we get Amy's sense of self, telling about Ollie, and
a clear description of their relationship (now and across time).

We return to *Same As It Ever Was* by Claire Lombardo to track
Julia's increasingly desperate relationship with an older

friend, Helen, who has shown her kindness. Julia is unmoored, a new mother with no connections or meaningful pursuits. She's spiraling the mental health drain when Helen comes along, offering a listening ear and sympathetic shoulder. When Helen goes away for a bit (before a larger rupture in the friendship, which is a big part of the story), Julia feels even worse and worries she's becoming over-reliant. This is how she characterizes the relationship at that point:

> She felt, for one of the first times since she'd started spending time with Helen, the familiar gaping hollow in her gut, dread, left once again alone with nothing but expanses of time and her own dull thoughts to entertain her. And she couldn't believe it, how instantaneously paler her life became without Helen and how pathetic that was. Helen was probably in the sky right now, drinking plane wine with her husband, glad to be free of the long roster of people who needed her, which most likely included Julia.[viii]

There's definitely a subset of this novel's target readership for whom this will be relatable (anxiety, anyone?). Julia loves what Helen offers and thinks herself "dull" and "hollow" without her new friend. This passage is a literary version of "Are you mad at me?" While this tells us about the relationship with Helen at face value, it's also about Julia's own shame, self-perception, inner struggle, and worldview: It's weak to need, she's "too much," and everyone is glad to be rid of her. Given how adrift she's been since having a kid, this tracks. But, as we've seen with other characters, like June from *Yellowface* in Chapter 6, what Julia needs isn't a friend. It's better self-esteem. (And as we saw in the other excerpt from this novel, also in Chapter 6, she eventually finds it!)

The following two passages come from *Bright Young Women* by Jessica Knoll, a fantastic multi-timeline literary novel with an ensemble cast. Pamela is a buttoned-up sorority girl whose friendship with Denise ends when someone sneaks into their house and violently murders her more outgoing counterpart. Left to deal with the wreckage and try to solve the murder, Pamela feels ill-suited to the task. As she gets more in touch with her emotions, she must also request help and support for, perhaps, the first time in her life. This is how she characterizes her relationship with her mother, who is, unfortunately, not able to give Pamela what she needs:

> On the other end of the phone, I heard my mother weeping. We had been performing the same dance all our lives—one in which I asked for little and received even less—but that was the moment I changed the steps on her. She never quite caught up, but she did try.[ix]

Pamela goes from "[asking] for little and [receiving] even less"—which is, by the way, a fantastic way of explaining an entire relationship in one short sentence—to demanding Mom see her and care for her. Despite Pamela leaving this exchange disappointed, she does manage to stand up for herself and change the steps of "the same dance" they'd been doing "all [their] lives." For someone bolder, this would be a tiny moment. For Pamela, it's a big win.

However, she's challenged elsewhere as well, especially when it comes to her own self-esteem in the context of her relationship with Denise. Roger, Denise's scummy ex-boyfriend and an early murder suspect, and Pamela have a fight at one point. He yells:

> "You sure get off on telling people what to do,

CHAPTER 7

Pamela. Denise was so sick of you. You know that? So
goddamn sick of you."

    I knew she was. I saw it in the petulant set of her
jaw every time I asked her to turn down Fleetwood
Mac on a school night, or reprimanded her for
touching the thermostat because inflation was through
the roof and I was trying to keep the electricity bill
down. *What happened to you?* she muttered just a week
before she died, when I caught her adding more than
the allotted two tablespoons of milk to her coffee.
Denise had made no secret of being sick of me, but
still, it hurt to hear it from someone who had treated
her so poorly.[x]

I love this excerpt because there are a number of things going
on. We have Roger saying something hurtful to Pamela,
which is external conflict. This is also a glimpse into *their*
relationship (or lack thereof). The dialogue relays the painful
idea that Denise—Pamela's best friend—was actually sick of
her and likely talking to Roger about it behind her back.
Worse, we get Pamela's admission that the criticism rings
true.

This is bolstered by a series of summarized mini-flashbacks
between the girls, as Pamela acted uptight and Denise
pushed back: *"What happened to you?"* This isn't a full scene
rendered with setting, dialogue, sensory detail, action, etc.,
but it gives readers a flavor of the weeks leading up to
Denise's death.

And wrapping it all together is Pamela's self-assessment.
Audiences might get the sense that she knows what she's like
—or at least how she's acting—and she might not enjoy it, but
she doesn't know how to change it. Of course, seeing all of
this come out with Roger, who "treated [Denise] so poorly" is
salt on a rather deep and nasty personal and interpersonal

wound. This particular snippet is an especially heavy-hitting 129 words.

I'll end this chapter on another summary of character relationships that's also wrapped around a mini-flashback. You'll notice the dialogue is, once again, embedded in the recollection rather than played out in full scene, and we'll talk more about this technique in the following chapter.

This sample comes from *Blue Sisters* by Coco Mellors. While we've already seen some character studies from this novel, the plot is really about three sisters—Avery, Bonnie, and Lucky—who are floundering in the aftermath of the fourth sister's death. We never get a chance to inhabit Nicky's POV, even though some of the other sisters' chapters go back in time to when she was still alive.

This means we can only learn about Nicky through the others' perspectives (explanations of her and their individual relationships) and Nicky's own dialogue and actions. The following is in Lucky's POV as she remembers a fight they had:

> Twenty and twenty-two, they had their worst fight ever after Lucky got drunk at Nicky's graduation party and accidentally set fire to the hair of one of the three girls in attendance ... She was sure they judged her for not graduating from high school. Try spending five years warding off the advances of grabby photographers, jealous attacks from other models, and constant inquiries into your weight and diet from agents, she wanted to tell them. *That* was an education. In the bathroom, Nicky splashed Lucky's face with water. *When did you get so boring?* Lucky slurred over the sink. Nicky grabbed her shoulders and shook her until her skull rattled. *There is nothing wrong with wanting to be normal!* she shouted. The next night, their

parents had plans to take them all out to dinner to celebrate, but Nicky told them she was never speaking to Lucky again. *Okay*, their mother said. *But the reservation is for seven P.M., so can you stop speaking to her after that?* They ended up splitting dessert.[xi]

From the excerpt in Chapter 5, we know Lucky is a self-proclaimed exceptional hot mess. She was even before Nicky died because she was thrust into the problematic underbelly of the high fashion modeling world from a young age. Once she feels her expiration date approaching (as there are, unfortunately, fewer old models in circulation) and her drinking and drug use ramps up, she's more lost than ever. We can see the roots of this dysfunction and Lucky's insecurity in the above memory, as she postures that her "School of Hard Knocks: Modeling Edition" education is more valid than Nicky's friends' traditional paths.

This is an ideological divide: Lucky wants everyone to know she's proud of herself, warts and all, and Nicky just wants to be *normal*. We also get a cameo from the sisters' mother, who seems to only care about maintaining appearances (and dinner reservations). And then, of course, despite the vicious fight and the big words ("Nicky told them she was never speaking to Lucky again"), they're sharing dessert just a few hours later. This is the mysterious and confusing bond of their specific sisterhood. Through telling, we traverse the entire spectrum of it in one paragraph.

I'm now going to take a major pivot from character to plot. The following chapter unpacks seven commonly used plot tentpole moments, which I've distilled from my reading of many popular frameworks, theories, and writing reference books. My goal here is to get you thinking about the structure of your story and what events you might want to include, and how showing and telling applies to major story ingredients and scene beats.

8

PLOT, CONFLICT, AND STAKES

As we consider how to link characters to the larger story, let's get into an overview of plot. Over the years, I've pulled together several well-known outline frameworks (everything from Story Grid to Save the Cat to Story Solution) and identified seven main tentpoles that most fiction (and some memoir) structures tend to follow. You might want to think about including some version of the following in your narratives:

- **Inciting Incident**: An event early in the plot which ramps up stakes and gets readers invested in the character and story. The first major conflict in your structure, the inciting incident changes the character's status from normal to abnormal in a way that creates tension which they—and the reader—become invested in resolving. This is a "one-way door" in the narrative, because once a character engages with the inciting incident, there's usually no going back to how things were. This event asks a lot of your protagonist internally. They may be reluctant to get involved at first, but they do so anyway (or there's no story).

- **Escalating Obstacles**: This is a large swath of the plot which covers parts of the first and second acts, if you're working with a traditional three-act structure. Emotionally, it's the gradual yet steady slide into despair as your character attempts to achieve their objective, fails, realizes they have growth to do, struggles with said growth, grapples with their vulnerability, and otherwise goes from confident to insecure. Driven by their objective and misbelief, they generally aren't aware of the extent of their internal struggle, the power wielded by the antagonist, the flimsiness of their plan, or all of the above. This section strips away their hopes that the solution to their conflict will come quickly and easily, or that they'll be able to succeed without changing or sacrificing some of the personal misbeliefs and flaws which brought them to conflict's doorstep in the first place. Of course, there should be some victories embedded in this sequence to encourage characters and entertain readers, or it'll be a slog.

- **Midpoint**: Many writers struggle with the "muddy middle" of a manuscript because it can be easy to clearly visualize the beginning, climax, and ending, but the rest of the story can resemble an opaque gray mist. One way around this plotting obstacle is to approach the midpoint from the perspective of character development. It's actually a very crucial moment in most narratives—when pretensions and illusions fall away and the true nature of the conflict and protagonist's vulnerability is revealed. (To them, at least. Readers who've been paying attention can usually see more than your character does at this juncture.) It may take protagonists a bit longer to realize the gravity of what's to come, as conflicts and stakes escalate toward the climax. The midpoint requires humility and courage in equal parts. Surrounding this sequence will be false victories, defeats, and other developments which test your protagonist's mettle, including relationship changes, allies falling away, and the deaths (literal or figurative) of old guides and ideas. The midpoint is also when the character begins to realize what's holding them back and the effect their wounds and needs have had on their present behavior, choices, and experiences.

- **Crisis**: There's often an "Act II crisis" in story structure where a protagonist is truly tested before they're cleared for the final battle. This is like a run-up to the climax, where things hang in the balance but the character flounders or doubts themselves, going back to old patterns without quite nailing the transition from pursuing their want to tackling their need. You'll want to start generously devastating them after the midpoint and before they reach the next stage of the conflict.

- **Dark Night of the Soul**: Tension is highest leading up to this character development point, which generally precedes or coincides with the climax. As the protagonist approaches the most high-stakes and dangerous (physically, emotionally, or both) moment in the story, they take stock. Whether they crumple in self-doubt, a plan is pulled out from under them, or a betrayal rocks their sense of what they believe to be true, this is a final test they must overcome from within. The Dark Night of the Soul is their only remaining chance to either back out or scrape themselves together for one last effort.

- **Synthesis Climax**: The character just did deep inquiry and resolved to give the conflict their all. Now, they're surprised to learn they can actually triumph by marshaling what was once perceived as their weakness. The protagonist, using all of their spark, wherewithal, and even reframed flaws, has been engaging with the plot in new ways since the midpoint. They synthesize the virtuous and problematic parts of themselves to claim victory or, at the very least, a new level of selfhood which they never would've achieved otherwise. If this sounds like a cheesy "the magic was inside them all along" moral, that's actually spot on. While you'd never overtly explain it this way in a novel or memoir worth its storytelling salt, this tentpole is all about the character realizing they're enough during the most dire circumstances of your plot.

- **Ending**: In most instances, your protagonist will eventually triumph. They'll sacrifice, suffer losses, and reach deeper into themselves than ever before, but they *will* triumph. If they don't, you're technically writing a tragedy, and that's all fine and good, as long as it's intentional. The final image of your project generally echoes the beginning, comes full circle, or reverses expectations. It also creates a sense of how the character might move forward in the short- and medium-term in the reader's mind. Your protagonist will have other conflicts, they'll still fail and flounder, but once they've achieved synthesis, solved the present conflict, and somewhat resolved their need and wound, they're much better prepared for anything else the future brings. If engineered well, the climax and ending bring everything together, and all of the turbulence and trouble you've created for the protagonist seems worth it to both character and reader. Goals are realized (or not), stakes come to pass (or don't), relationships are ironed out (for the most part), and the character reaches a new level of mastery or understanding of themselves and their lives. The inner struggle crests and resolves (though maybe not in the way audiences and the protagonist expected), and readers leave more or less emotionally satisfied (even if you're planning a series).

As you construct a story from the above components, your mission is to make more meaning from them. Not only should you use telling to clearly portray what's happening and why (if appropriate), but for emotional context as well. Why does this event matter? What does this mean in the larger context of the story or world (which we'll talk about in Chapter 10)? How does the event affect the character (the stakes, which we'll discuss in a moment)?

Don't just put the plot point in your manuscript and leave the significance up to readers entirely. How a character reacts, what they do to update or change their existing plan, and how they pursue their goal as a result—once the ramifications of an event reveal themselves—are all great things to tell.

You can use interiority (let's say the character takes a beat after an intense fight sequence to count the bodies and change strategies), action, or dialogue to support key plot points, especially since you want to convey they're happening in a cause-and-effect fashion for maximum storytelling cohesion.

For example, a character attempts to woo their enemy to access the family's vault, only to be rejected. Now they need a new plan. They recalibrate their understanding of the situation and notice a servant's entrance they might never have seen if they hadn't been trying to entice the villain into the bedroom. The next scene might find them in a maid's uniform, getting one step closer to the antagonist's inner sanctum. Evaluating how a plot point went, comparing that to the objective or need (scene-specific or story-wide), and creating a new plan of attack are all great topics for some telling and additional context.

Here are some more granular plot components and external character benchmarks which you might find yourself using. Below each are suggestions for conveying them with both showing and telling:

- **Timeline**:
  - TELL to orient the reader efficiently. ("Three years ago, she left without saying goodbye. Now she was at my door.")
  - SHOW when the emotional fallout lingers in behavior, flashback, or metaphor, e.g., reacting poorly to a similar departure. Showing the timeline unfolding is also how you're going to execute your plot.
- **Setups for plot payoff**:
  - TELL to plant a narrative seed clearly and quickly. ("She'd always wanted to go to Mars—just not like this.")
  - SHOW the recurring desire or fear playing out later in high-stakes scenes.
- **Turning points and realizations**:
  - TELL internal realizations that can't be dramatized efficiently. ("That's when she knew—he'd never loved her, not really.")
  - SHOW external shifts in behavior or decisions which reflect the realization. This is the effect of the stimulus, either as it's happening or after.
- **Cause-and-effect logic**:
  - TELL when connecting dots the reader might miss. ("It wasn't the lie that broke her—it was that he didn't flinch while telling it.")

- SHOW the impact in the next plot point or character growth moment, which *could only* happen because of the previous scene.
- **Shifts in motivation or goal:**
  - TELL to flag a turning point in desire. ("Now it wasn't about proving them wrong—it was about surviving.")
  - SHOW the new strategy reflected in how they act, who they push away, or what they risk.
- **Time jumps and transitional moments:**
  - TELL to summarize unimportant in-between happenings. ("The next two weeks passed in a blur of hospital light.")
  - SHOW the emotional residue afterward— weariness, distance, numbness.
- **Secrets and revelations:**
  - TELL to drop a bomb. ("She wasn't just his mortal enemy. She was his sister.")
  - SHOW the tension build-up before and the reaction after—not just the reveal itself.
- **Decline or spiral:**
  - TELL to compress repetitive events which convey similar ideas. ("She stopped returning calls. Then texts. Then emails.")
  - SHOW key moments that make the spiral feel earned—snapshots of refusal, loss, or apathy.
- **Stakes:**
  - TELL when the reader needs clarity on why something matters. ("If he lost the case, his daughter went back to her mother.")
  - SHOW emotional reactions, escalating risks, other characters reacting to the same threat. You can and should also show throughout why those stakes matter to the protagonist specifically.
- **Offscreen events:**

- ○ TELL to catch the reader up on things the character learned or did off-page, as long as your POV access allows you to know. ("While she considered what she really wanted, he'd already bought the ring.")
- ○ SHOW how those events, if they're never dramatized on the page, ripple forward: surprise, emotional payoff.
- **Logistical moves**:
  - ○ TELL to keep momentum tight, since overly detailed play-by-play can slow the action. ("They took the train to Paris and found the contact at the bar.")
  - ○ SHOW when the journey involves tension— suspense, delay, a dead end, or obstacle *en route*.

We'll look at some plot-relevant showing and telling excerpts next.

From the Shelves

Here are some examples of key in-the-moment plot revelations or after-the-moment reactions on the page. I'm not able to reproduce entire scenes with major plot points, but in the following section, you'll get a sense of how telling can support the external moments you'll be weaving into your stories. Let's start with a few small external benchmarks which carry significant weight. Notice how they're summarized and how the relevant characters react.

The first is from the literary novel *Grown Women* by Sarai Johnson, which follows three generations from the same family. Corinna, who was "raised better than that," goes and gets herself pregnant by a teen boy who has no intention of sticking around. In the below passage, she has just finished summarizing how they slipped into having sex on the downlow, though he never deigned to treat her like she mattered to him in public. She reveals her pregnancy, Johnny promptly skips town, and she reacts:

> When Johnny and the Cadillac were gone, Corinna pressed the heels of her hands against her eyes in a futile attempt to keep the tears from coming. In a different universe, maybe she and Johnny might have been something vaguely resembling a family. Johnny's rejection felt like a loss, but only because she allowed herself to believe they'd had anything at all. But now she did have something; she had a baby, her very *own* baby, to grow and love. In light of this revelation, Corinna decided that she would only cry this one time over Johnny. Then she would let it go. Move on. Get over it.[i]

You could write several chapters about Corinna confronting Johnny, his rejection, and her response. Instead, we get it summarized in an efficient way. She goes from having nothing (in terms of a relationship with Johnny) to having a baby "to grow and love." Corinna completely changes her worldview and attitude in the span of a few sentences, whereas in the hands of another writer, this growth arc could easily be stretched out for an entire novel about a teen's first heartbreak.

Characters on the brink of big decisions are perfectly positioned to collide with plot points. How a protagonist interacts with external conflict, how they approach a turning point, and what they choose to do makes the internal external. It can also make characters proactive. While the plot will sometimes serve up conflict seemingly randomly (a visitor at the door, a car accident, getting fired, or finding out about a cheating spouse), protagonists can connect with external events and try to regain control of their stories with choices.

Here's an example from the fabulously weird Appalachian gothic novel *The Bog Wife* by Kay Chronister, which features a family that's either cursed or chosen—it's tough to determine which—to be the keepers of a bog. As a reward for their bog-tending, they will be given a bog wife for the oldest son, a woman made from magic and mud. Wenna is the only family member who has escaped their sheltered existence, but when a bog wife fails to materialize and her father gets ill, she has to return. In the process, she quits her job and breaks up with her partner, so there's not much waiting for her in the outside world. Soon, she's sucked into the toxic family dynamic just as easily as bones are absorbed by the bog. Once Dad dies, she must decide whether to stay and help her siblings, or if she has the stomach to escape again (but to what?):

> So Wenna could not go back to Illinois. And she did not know where else to go. With a nagging sensation that she was slowly sinking down into depths from which she would not rise again, she stayed through the last rainstorms of the summer, through the first cranberry harvest of autumn (meager and too early, a shadow of the harvests she remembered in childhood, producing only a few buckets of wizened dark berries that were too sour for raw consumption), and finally even through peat-cutting at the end of September.[ii]

The plot has presented her with a tipping point—a choice. She must decide how much more of her family's dysfunction she can stomach. Notice how she's already pushing the timeline back—she stays for the summer, then autumn, and now it's time to cut the peat. In just a few sentences, we move the story forward to her next decision—whether to stay for a devastating and isolating winter.

Up next is an example of a character, Emily, gearing up to bury the body of a backpacker she and her friend, Kathryn, killed by accident (or so she believes) in the thriller *We Were Never Here* by Andrea Bartz. Notice how she talks herself into it, and contextualizes what it might feel like by comparing it to slipping into an alternate timeline, even though there's no speculative element in this novel:

> *This is a weird break from reality; you're about to slip into an alternate timeline and wormhole back when it's over. This is a project to be managed, a problem to be solved. Keep going. Keep going. Keep going.*[iii]

From the italics, you can tell this is all verbatim thought as she's coaching herself. We also get Emily's worldview: "this is a project to be managed, a problem to be solved." This tells readers a lot about the type of person she is. She never expected to be burying a body, so she slides into denial to get it done. The close first-person POV almost sounds like a mantra, immersing audiences in a spiraling thought loop and providing an immediate feeling of panic and drive. This is the kind of self-talk or narrative voice that works really well when it's applied to (or surrounds) any kind of action or danger.

Next, we'll ratchet things up a notch with two excerpts from different upmarket thrillers. These are in-the-moment renderings of characters who are facing their respective Dark Night of the Soul or Synthesis Climax moments.

The first comes from *Look in the Mirror* by Catherine Steadman and features the POV character of Maria, who we previously met in Chapter 5. She's survived a lot in her life, from being a migrant to working full-time while going to medical school, and now she's being hunted by a shadowy group of antagonists. As the bad guys close in, she reacts:

> Maria feels sick at the cleanness of it all and a new anger begins to rise inside her, an anger at the idea that her pain could be so easily deleted, hidden, erased.
> *Well, I will not make it that easy. Oh no.*
> Maria will get her murderer's blood and hair and cells under her nails and take him with her if she can. She will make their plan an impossibility. And even if she has to die herself just to fuck them over, she will.[iv]

At face value, "Maria feels sick" is obvious telling. She also feels "anger." But think about the surrounding context. A killer is upon her. These might be the last moments of her life. The author has decided to stop being precious and focus, instead, on the raw feelings of rage as Maria fights back. She doesn't see memories flash before her eyes or get sentimental about loved ones. Instead, she almost seems okay with death. All she cares about is not making it easy—and making her death, if it must happen, mean something. That's the focus of this scene, and it fits the character's voice, so the author has decided to be direct and tell.

Writers in "show, don't tell" mode might argue that the word "anger" appears multiple times! But this isn't lazy repetition —it's cumulative escalation. Look at how it builds: "a new anger begins to rise" is the recognition of anger; then "even if she has to die herself just to fuck them over" is the apotheosis of that anger turning into purpose. This is not a thesaurus problem—the author knows other words to express the feeling. This is a character leveling up emotionally, and the repetition is rhythmic, purposeful, and voice-infused. (Also, let's not pretend "anger" is some rookie red flag when it's surrounded by powerhouse ideas and voice like "get her murderer's blood and hair and cells under her nails.")

Shouldn't Maria show this emotion instead of just stating it? Showing only works when the emotion is unclear. In this case, the emotion *is* the plot. The author doesn't need to show Maria pacing or hyperventilating. That would delay the insight we're meant to get here: The protagonist is about to do something reckless, self-sacrificial, and maybe brilliant. Sometimes, you don't want emotional ambiguity. You want emotional certainty. And telling is the sharpest tool to deliver it.

Rather than pearl-clutching over "feels" or "anger," ask yourself:

- Is the emotion clear and specific?
- Does the telling reveal character logic?
- Is the voice alive in how the emotion is delivered?
- Does it move the story forward?

If yes? Congratulations. You're not being lazy—you're being precise, "angry" or not.

A similar moment happens in the thriller *All the Other Mothers Hate Me* by Sarah Harman, as unlikely hero (maybe even anti-hero) Florence has tracked a kidnapper to his hideout. While this chapter *also* includes a confrontation with the antagonist, Adam, this is a quieter moment when we bridge the high-stakes external conflict with how Florence feels about it all using telling. Yes, this is a cliché mirror scene, but in this instance, it's used to track her sense of self and character development, so it does double duty:

> In the filthy mirror, I examine my own reflection. My makeup is gone now, and my eyes are puffy and swollen, still stinging from the soap. Wet hair clings to my skull like limp spaghetti. The gash on my head is bleeding again. I look like a monster. I feel like a

>   monster. Small and wrong and bad. Adam saw it. *Dark*
>   *recognizing dark.* That's why he's asked me and not
>   Jenny to help him.
>
>   I dry my face with a stiff towel and tuck the cool
>   plastic syringe back into the band at the center of my
>   bra. My eyes linger on the grimy mirror. For a moment,
>   I see someone else. Not a monster. But someone who
>   doesn't care how she looks anymore. Who doesn't
>   have to care. The goddess Medusa, dangerous,
>   powerful in her hideousness.[v]

As she psychs herself up to attack Adam and try to rescue the kidnapped child, she must make herself feel capable of such an insane task. She might even have to kill Adam, so she needs to tell herself she's "a monster." She's "dark," the same as Adam, and therefore she can do dark things when she needs to. And it works. She finds this grim pep talk inspiring and can face what's next.

Over the course of two tight, expository paragraphs, we see Florence go from "small and wrong and bad" to "dangerous [and] powerful in her hideousness." Then she saves the day because she has talked herself out of her human desire to "care," a strategic pivot done for the greater good.

Many writing teachers would tell you that "I feel like a monster" is bad writing. And they might be right. But in this moment, the telling weaves plot climax and character transformation together and serves a clear function.

The process of making meaning from a story's plot rests on to the concept of stakes. Because the stakes answer the all-important question of, "Why does this event/character development/new piece of information *matter*?"

And not just to characters, but, by proxy, to readers as well. That's what we'll explore in the final section of this chapter, in addition to conflict (what the plot creates for the character) and tension (the protagonist's inner experience as a result).

The examples in the following section speak to the real challenge of this guide and demonstrating how to use telling in spectacular ways, not just for efficiency.

Conflict, Tension, and Stakes

Plot is a carefully orchestrated sequence of ups and downs, expectation shifts, inner struggles, and external sources of conflict. All of these create tension and stakes. My favorite tool to keep you unpacking the emotion of any external development is a simple two-question prompt: "And? So?"

I can't get fired from this job.

And?

If I do, I won't be able to afford daycare for my kid.

So?

I'll have to become a stay-at-home mom.

And?

I worry I'll lose myself.

So?

Just like what happened to *my* mom growing up.

Here, I'm showcasing the deeper pain and conflict below a relatively common worry: getting fired. And, to be clear, I'm not saying that staying home to raise kids is going to elicit

131

this reaction from everyone. Some people love it. But for *this specific character*, it's frightening. Perhaps she watched the light go out of her mother when *she* had to leave her job and raise children instead. In our modern culture, this can happen, and it tends to put certain pressures on the primary caretaker, whether or not they have a partner. It's absolutely possible to love raising kids, but if someone isn't predisposed to this role, or if it's not something they initially chose for themselves, there could be tension.[1]

Whether you agree with this specific character's fear or not, it's undeniable that "I can't handle my own light going out, just like Mom's did" is much more specific than "I don't want to get fired." Our fears and worst-case scenarios tend to be finely detailed. (Even our best-case scenarios, though those are less frequently explored in storytelling outside of the character's initial objective and motivation.)

This is why it can be perfectly okay—desirable, even—to tell about conflict, tension, and stakes. Ideally, you will have also established character, objective, motivation, backstory, wound, and need as additional context. Sometimes through showing, sometimes through telling. When we reach *this* moment of conflict for *this* character, we will likely already know:

- Whether her identity hinges on work, and why;
    - This makes the notion of losing her job even more painful.
- The backstory of her childhood, maybe with an eye

---

1. To be honest, I hesitated in making the example character a woman because that tends to be the default when we think about child-rearing, but if this is a multi-generational conflict, it invariably rings more true if these are female characters because it's even less likely that a father would've stayed home decades ago.

toward developing Mom as a beloved but distant parent; and

- Maybe Mom even left the family because she couldn't take the pressure of her role, as Grace did in the *Amazing Grace Adams*, excerpted in Chapter 6.

- Her desires and needs, both professional and personal.
    - And which of these would be threatened if she lost her job or was forced into a complete identity 180.

With all of this existing information operating in harmony through showing and telling, we can more easily threaten what's important to the character, add dimension to the present conflict using an understanding of the past, and make the current plot situation matter in a big way.

If you've done all of the above groundwork for the protagonist, you won't need to do much explaining when it comes to conflict, tension, and stakes in the moment. For example, any time this character goes into the office setting, readers will be on high alert for trouble, since they'll already know how important her career is to her.

This is the great thing about telling. You might have a hell of a mental, emotional, and philosophical block to get over before you feel comfortable exploring it, but once you do, you can accomplish more with less. Go ahead and tell the detail, then trust readers to retain it. The next time this part of the story is relevant, you won't have to do the work again.

From the Shelves

Up next are several examples of telling about stakes. The first comes from *The Hunter's Daughter* by Nicola Solvinic, the thriller about a woman whose dad is a serial killer, originally explored in Chapter 5. Anna is currently working in law enforcement and encounters Agent Parkes, the man who caught her dad years ago. She last saw him when she was a little girl, so odds of him recognizing her are slim, but she makes sure to spell out the exact ramifications and what it would mean to be identified now, using telling to bolster the stakes:

> Did he know? No, there was no way he could. It was my imagination. If he recognized me, my life would be destroyed. My career would evaporate, and this investigation would be blown to smithereens due to my conflict of interest. I'd have to go on the run, hounded by press. And Nick … he'd know what a monster I really was.[vi]

Direct interiority is used here to project emotional exposure and outline the potential professional consequences if anyone connects the dots between Anna and her father. This telling creates character-generated suspense and spells out the worst-case scenario so readers know, without a doubt, what she *doesn't* want. (This explanation also suggests what she *does* want: to stay hidden, avoid the press, keep her nose down, and remain a private citizen with a secret.) There are multiple character and plot layers explored and reinforced in just a few sentences.

In the following excerpt, we have a global catastrophe on our hands, but readers get to see it play out through the perspective of the uber-uber-*uber*-wealthy Will, Ellen, and their family. Forget the doomsday prepper backyard bunker and musty ration cans. Instead, think of an off-grid private island and a jet ready to scramble at a moment's notice. This is the premise of *The Future* by Naomi Alderman. When the alarm sounds and the apocalypse unfolds (the novel doesn't clarify the nature of these events), these wealthy characters must mobilize their worst-case scenario plans. In this short scene, the stakes of keeping their escape a secret are defined in the context of Ellen wanting to call her child, Badger, and include them:

> Will gave Ellen a sharp look. Badger was their youngest, their non-binary child with a radical political stance. Badger had mentioned several times that they did not approve of this whole system, of warnings and private jets and hidden safe bunkers in New Zealand.
>
> The protocol was to make no phone calls in this situation. It was no use having a safe and comfortable place to ride out a global catastrophe if everyone knew you were leaving and could follow you. Get the doors sealed before anyone knew you'd left—that was the plan. Still.
>
> "Call Badger," said Ellen.
>
> An agony of thudding heartbeats before Badger answered the call. Their face, projected onto the wall of the suite, was very close to their screen—they never wanted their mother to see where they were. How sharper than a serpent's tooth it is.
>
> Still, Badger looked afraid. This gave Ellen a certain grim satisfaction. See? Your mother still does know something worth knowing.[vii]

Not only do we get a peek at a world in crisis, but we learn about Ellen's relationship with Badger. There's obviously conflict here. Badger disapproves of these doomsday games on political and anti-capitalist grounds. They have also gone to great lengths—as we're told—to maintain family boundaries. Readers get the sense that mother and child haven't talked in a while. But Ellen's fear for Badger overpowers her and her willingness to adhere to the plan. This omniscient-leaning third-person voice tells us exactly how Ellen feels—but it works because of the emotional contrast between Badger's fear and Ellen's feeling of validation and justification. It's blunt and judgmental on purpose.

Badger left but now they're scared. This is a very strange time to feel "grim satisfaction," but Ellen nails the moment home with: "See? Your mother still does know something worth knowing." That phrase right there could well encapsulate many teen- or twentysomething-parent relationships. It's also a blend of Ellen's narration and interiority. While we do get dialogue, scene, and action here, a lot of the world-building, rules, and, especially, stakes are told.

Will Ellen break her own protocol and invite Badger into the bunker? Or will this deviation from the plan cost them their opportunity to reach sanctuary? Readers become more grounded in the urgency of the moment as well.

Here's another example from *Vera Wong's Unsolicited Advice for Murderers* by Jesse Q. Sutanto. Another POV character, Sana, is part of an ensemble cast doing a DIY murder investigation. She has been posing as a true crime podcaster but worries that Julia, Marshall's widow (the one with the nice ass, from Chapter 1), is about to learn the truth:

> Oh god. Entire star systems are exploding inside Sana. She needs to come up with an excuse to stop Julia, but she can't, her mind a complete blank, she's not a writer like her mother, who by now would've come up with at least five different legit excuses as to why Julia won't find her nonexistent podcast online. Powerless, Sana watches as Julia takes out her phone and swipes to unlock it. Here it comes, she's going to

be exposed as a complete fraud, and then the suspicion will come, and maybe then they'll even find out how she's been following Marshall for weeks.[viii]

We get Sana's interiority as she watches Julia potentially search for her (nonexistent) podcast. Notice how the language supports this as a high-tension, high-stakes moment.

The last example, from a funny YA horror novel (yes, this is an oxymoron), *The Blonde Dies First* by Joelle Wellington, even outright mentions high stakes. It's enough to send English teachers to the school nurse for a cool washcloth, but here, it works because the voice is direct and the entire story is a send-up of the slasher genre. Devon, the main character, explains:

> Except the stakes are higher. They mean more, and that means the confidence we're channeling is unshakable. And for the briefest of moments and for the first time ever, I'm jealous of Yaya.
> I only wish they would have that kind of confidence in me. That I had that confidence in me.[ix]

There are a few additional details which help support this dry statement of stakes. While there *is* a murderer on the loose, the real conflict is emotional, identity-based, and relational. Devon knows her friends support her, which means she doesn't want to let them down. Worse, she doesn't feel confident, so she worries their faith in her is misplaced. At face value, Devon is right: the stakes *are* higher. But the layers the author included offer a deeper frequency of resonance, too.

Now you've learned how to support character and plot with elements of both showing *and* telling. This brings up the idea of scene versus summary, and how to leverage these

techniques to craft a compelling story. The next chapter will
act as a little palate cleanser and exploration of how you can
weave both narration and overview together into your
structure. The chapter you just read offered a broad overview
of the *what* of plot. The following chapter explores the *how*.

9

SUMMARY AND SCENE

If you've been following my writing guides for any length of time, you know I originally started the conversation of showing *and* telling in *Writing Interiority*. In that book, I explored—to the tune of about 600 pages worth of material, with approximately 30,000 words of excerpts, and yes, even *I* was tired of hearing my own voice by the end, but I literally couldn't stop—how to get into the inner world of the character, including thoughts, feelings, reactions, expectations, and inner struggles. And I still fully believe and would literally stake my career on the importance of interiority, as many writers have a hard time closing the narrative distance and achieving this kind of deep POV access.

This is a less common issue, but some writers get so deep into their characters and interiority that they neglect action and forward momentum. This problem—too much interiority, too much thinking and exposition—can be a difficult one to address. The challenge becomes stepping out of a skull and into a story. But how?

All that character development needs a structure to support it. Enter: the plot. At the bare minimum, you can apply the advice in the action and dialogue sections from Chapter 3. Instead of relying solely on interiority, you have two characters *discussing* themselves and one another. It's dialogue, it's scene, there are dialogue tags and action tags, and the characters might even be *doing* something: whispering during a meeting; talking to their seat mate on a long-haul flight; reconnecting over drinks at a trendy bar; chatting on the phone; waiting for the movie to start, etc.

So what's the problem?

None of these actions are very dynamic, first of all. And while they take place during a situation, they are not plot. Review the above ideas. Everything the characters are *doing* in those examples involves … sitting down. Think about the eventual movie of your story. (Why the hell not? We can dream big. But this isn't a delusion of grandeur, it's actually a helpful mental exercise you can use when you're writing and suspect you've gotten too internal.)

There are really only two analogues for this kind of "scene" in film. First, and most obvious, is voiceover. We show the character sitting and thinking (sitting again!), looking into the mirror and thinking, waiting for their smoothie to be ready at the juice bar and thinking, engaging in some kind of activity … and thinking. The second way to render interiority in film would be a montage. The character is training or having a makeover or falling in love. Maybe we learn the contents of their thoughts as this is unspooling, but we can also simply see a period of intense transformation portrayed visually. Montages are used for turning points, commitments or recommitments, life-changing decisions or revelations, and other moments which anchor character development.

In a musical, you can also convey interiority in song. In fact, look at how many stage and film musical songs are used to make characters explore their identity; state their dreams, needs or goals; contextualize a relationship; express their worldview, philosophy, or world; and mark character change.

Think about the last movie, musical, or movie musical you saw, though. These moments of character self-expression are few and far between. Yes, musicals have a lot of songs, but not every single one is about the character's inner struggle or sense of self. There are action scenes and numbers meant to flat-out entertain.

If we were to make a film of your manuscript, would it be mostly voiceover as the character sits around? This is a straightforward visual signal that you're not actually engaging in action. If this sounds like you, let's find some alternatives to add to your storytelling toolkit.

For example, if a daughter character's relationship with her dad is core to your story, you could certainly offer tons of stream-of-consciousness exploration of all facets of their troubled dynamic. But this could lead to a lot of interiority. Instead, work the circumstances into scenes. And not just one expository info-dump. An important relationship can and should play out across multiple chapters and interactions.

Put Dad and Daughter in scene together and see what they have to say, how they say it, and how they treat one another. Is Dad bitter that his life didn't turn out as he wanted? Does he cast undue blame on his daughter for being hindered from pursuing his dreams? Does he fixate on slights and betrayals—real and imagined—from the past, rather than making an effort to see her for who she is in the present? How does this dynamic inform their behavior? Or their actions? Does he promise to meet her for lunch, then leave her hanging? Sometimes a character's absence communicates just as much—if not more—than their presence. By putting them into scene, we create in-the-moment plot conflict instead of static information about their troubled relationship.

And when it comes to rendering action on the page, we have two primary approaches at our disposal: summary and scene.

Summary

As we've already discussed, you can, indeed, summarize certain character components, like backstory, wound, need, objective, and more. The real art and craft of plotting involves first figuring out what to include in your story, then *how* you'll do it.

In *Writing Irresistible First Pages*, I unpacked several story-beginning clichés. Perhaps the most well-known is starting with a character waking up in the morning. Why? This is not a compelling subject for a first chapter because it unintentionally sends the message that the writer has no affinity for plot. If you're starting your story the same way most of us start our days, this telescopes to readers that you're not going to be selective about your story's events.

After all, if you start each chapter with a character waking up in the morning and end it with them going to bed, you're just taking us through "a day in life" of the protagonist. But not every single moment of a character's life is going to be story-worthy. This ties back to another note I find myself giving frequently, one against play-by-play choreography. This means the habit some writers have of transcribing every little movement a character makes.

My longstanding example is a woman making a sandwich. You can take two approaches to rendering this mundane task on the page. First, you can spell it all out, like this:

She walked to the refrigerator and plucked the mayonnaise from the top shelf. The lettuce and tomato were in the crisper and the turkey and cheese slices were in the deli drawer. The bread was already waiting on the cutting board. She unsheathed a knife from the block—serrated of course, for slicing through the thick-crust sourdough. With a laugh, she realized she'd forgotten a butter knife from the cutlery drawer for the spread.

At the wooden cutting board, she assembled her *mise en place*, then got to work, sawing hearty slabs from the loaf, her right arm burning from the exertion. Once that was done, she grabbed a plate from the cupboard, where she would arrange her creation…

Snore.

Sorry. I even lost myself there for a moment.

You get the point. If we transcribe this action detail by painstaking detail, we could easily spend an entire page on her making lunch. But is this necessary? On the other hand, we can summarize the above like this:

She made a sandwich.

Now, here's where you might want to apply some creative and intentional decision-making. Is this sandwich going to be important to the story? (I mean, if it's an ordinary sandwich, this is highly unlikely, but if she's about to poison her husband with arsenic-laced mayonnaise, we may want to spend a little time on the details.) If it's a singular, plot-worthy sandwich, you can reintroduce some selective interiority and marry the internal and external. Notice how, above, her mindset is missing from the meticulous logistical and spatial description.

But if this is a new and unexpected episode of sandwich-making, interiority is worth including. Our character, let's name her Kathryn, has never made *this* kind of sandwich before, which elevates the action to something plot-worthy. You could do something like:

> Kathryn paused in front of the refrigerator. Dutch's. His favorite. But it was missing a crucial ingredient. She glanced over her shoulder to make sure he was still rapt in front of the football game, his feet kicked up on the coffee table. Then she reached into her pocket for the small vial of arsenic. This would be risky, but she'd decided to chance it. With his heart issues—all that mayonnaise, no doubt—if she played her cards right, nobody would order a toxicology report.
>
> Besides, time was running out. If she heard him say, "Make me a sandwich, woman!" one more time, she might not be able to live with herself.
>
> She uncapped the vial and stirred the poison into the jar before smoothing a generous glob onto the sourdough. Oh, she'd make him a sandwich, all right. His last.

That's obviously one (macabre) way to elevate the action of making a sandwich with interiority and give it an important role in the story. It's not just external, and it's not merely internal. Now it matters, and you're weaving character and plot together. And, most importantly, this moment becomes part of a larger narrative.

Kathryn is likely having marital problems.[1] Instead of thinking about them or talking to friends about them (both of

---

1. You think?!

which can be passive), she's externalizing her thoughts and feelings with action, which also advances the larger plot. Not only is she *doing* something about her situation or circumstances, she's being proactive *and* setting up the chain of external events which might follow. What if this gambit works? What if it doesn't? Either way, there will be internal and external downstream effects.

If you're just working on something logistical—like a transition between scenes—or filling in the blanks for something that's meant to largely happen "off-screen," consider summarizing the relevant details instead. You could even omit the data and write a more significant transition.

For example, if Kathryn has a fight with her husband on Monday night but doesn't poison his food until the following Sunday, we might not even need to put the events of the intervening week on the page.[2] You could end their conflict on Monday night with something like:

> She knew she had to do something, she just didn't know what yet. Or when.

Then we can pick up the action on Sunday, and readers will be able to pick up the dots and fill in the blanks to assume she's been working on her plan all week.

Summary with transitions could help there, too:

> All week, Kathryn waited for her chemist friend to get back to her. Could he get her what she needed? He finally texted her on Friday, and they met at a coffee shop to make the exchange.

---

2. Also, if this is the case, why drag it out? Have them fight on Saturday night to keep tension high and pacing taut. You're making the whole thing up, including the calendar of events!

"Whatever you use this for," he told her, "make sure it doesn't get back to me."

"Of course," she said, pocketing the vial with a shaking hand.

Now she just had to find the right time to put her plan into action.

It's up to you how you want to bridge the events between Monday night and Sunday afternoon. What do readers need to know? The provenance of the arsenic? A developing romantic connection with the chemist friend? Then maybe we do need to play out the above scene in more detail, which we'll discuss in the following section. Or perhaps the few snippets of dialogue, similar to the above, would be sufficient for the time being, and you can develop more of a relationship with the chemist once the husband is—ahem—out of the picture. (Kathryn may be a murderer, but she's not a cheater!)

So is summary enough, or does it feel insufficient for a specific plot point you're envisioning? When you're working with important story moments, you'll want to expand them into full scene. Summary is fine, and I'll give you additional tools for deciding which plot events deserve a compressed treatment at the end of this chapter, but scenes combine into the actual meat of your story. Narration is the fullest possible external rendering of everything else you've created and are planning to include. We'll dig into what this means in practice below.

Scene

Full narrative often includes setting, character action, interiority, and dialogue. It has a beginning, middle, and end. Once the event plays out, the character finds themselves with their expectations reset, in a new situation, with a new plan of attack to set themselves up for their next scene, and having either triumphed or run into an obstacle. In essence, something has changed for the protagonist and in the story as a result of them participating in the plot point readers have just experienced.

When you decide you need to render your story in full scene, remember to take your time. This is the difference between summary and dramatization. Let's take a run at expanding the compressed narration about Kathryn and the chemist from the previous section. Consider what her expectations are going in, her experience in interiority as the scene unfolds, and where she stands afterward. You might do something like the following:

> Kathryn almost didn't go into the coffee shop. Sure, she'd come this far, and it felt like there was no going back already, because she'd involved Christopher. He knew. She could still back out … but then what?
>
> Returning to her life and being mistreated, day in, day out, until Bruce either died naturally or decided he was sick of making her existence a living hell? Would he ever leave, though? Or did he think she was his to boss around forever?
>
> No, she couldn't stay. She knew that. Kathryn couldn't lose her nerve now.
>
> She pushed through the door and was greeted by the acrid smell of dark roast, an edge of bitterness in the air. The espresso machine whirred away at the counter. She scanned the room. There was Christopher, sitting in the corner with a latte, staring at his laptop. Just another nondescript guy in a coffee shop, except she knew the truth.
>
> Kathryn beelined for him, her stomach cramping. She couldn't possibly get a coffee, even though she

knew she'd look more casual ordering one. A few people glanced up when she passed their tables, and she couldn't help thinking they knew somehow. Were her dark intentions clear on her face?

But nobody stopped her or said anything. For a second, she wished someone would. "You don't have to do this," the college student with blue hair and rose gold headphones could whisper. But nobody did.

She slid into the empty chair across from Christopher with a curt, "Hello."

"Hey, Kat."

The silence stretched between them, and she didn't know how to proceed. *Do you have the stuff?* No, this wasn't some seedy corner drug deal. Besides, she really didn't want to talk about it. Christoper didn't need her life story. The less he knew, after all, the better.

"I have your mail," he said, reaching into his laptop bag, extracting a padded envelope, and sliding it across the table.

It took her a moment to understand the game. "My ... oh, right. Thanks. *So weird* they keep delivering it to your address."

"Yeah." He studied her face, a question in his eyes.

"I'll ... I'll talk to the post office about it," she stammered, looking down at her hands. "But thanks. For this."

"No problem." Then he dropped his voice so low, she had to lean in to hear him. "This isn't going to get back to me, is it?"

"Of course not." Except she didn't know if she could make that promise. If any of this came to light, it would mean she'd gotten herself caught, and she honestly didn't know if she could hold up under interrogation. Better not to let herself think about *that*.

The scene could continue, with more reassurance from Kathryn, or gratitude to Christopher for his help. Or he might get spooked, pack up his laptop, and leave ... taking the arsenic with him. But we've now seen the event play out, which offered an opportunity for Kathryn to second-guess herself, recommit, and grapple with the potential ramifications ... for both of them.

Notice that I've included some scene-setting, dialogue, and interiority as she considers what's happening and the stakes. We have her and Christopher sizing one another up and some description of body language and action.

If her vacillation is important to convey to readers in this moment, this is a worthwhile scene to put on the page. Or maybe she's not nervous—she's excited. Instead of a scene with Christopher, maybe we go out to a wine bar that Friday with a girlfriend who's always hated Bruce. If Kathryn has confided[3] in this friend and revealed her plan, they could celebrate her impending "freedom" and make plans for a singles getaway. The tone of that exchange would be very different from the interaction we just read.

Or maybe we cut right to the sandwich-making scene.

It's up to you to decide not only what to include and when, but how detailed you want to get. You'll also notice that a scene is a commitment of energy and word count. When we play something out in full narrative, with all of the associated trappings, it takes up space in your manuscript. This pro or con, depending on your current draft, can help you decide how comprehensive you want to get. If your project is already straining at the word count expectations for your genre and

---

3. My wonderful editor, Amy Wilson, has reminded me that the first rule of murder is not chatting about it. But Kathryn is clearly not a criminal mastermind. And I think Amy might listen to too many true crime podcasts...

target audience, you may need to be more selective about your plotting and which components get the full scene treatment.

Alternatively, if your draft is running lean, this could be a signal to add more plot (or maybe a subplot or two) and character development, as well as more scene-work. If you have room to grow, consider which moments in your story could use comprehensive real-time rendering. Where is the emotional juice, currently? Are you leaving any opportunities on the table to get readers even more engaged?

Audiences tend to gravitate toward scene over summary because it goes deeper into the character's interiority, showcases relationships through action on the page, and offers more immersive setting and sensory details.

Think of the difference between that movie training montage and an exchange that takes five full minutes of screen time. We can gloss over the particulars, or we can take a pause and sink into a sustained moment of story. What effect do you want to have on your audience with each piece of your plot puzzle?

A scene is a web of decisions, dynamics, context, and emotion —and you can use both showing and telling to sharpen tension, deepen stakes, or move things along. Scene is just a container—and inside it, you're making constant decisions about what to dramatize and what to declare.

Below is a list of some common scene ingredients and what you might tell and show about each:

- **What the character thinks:**
  - TELL when a thought transitions or clarifies. ("She knew she'd regret this. She said yes anyway.")
  - SHOW thoughts through hesitation, missteps, or

contradiction. ("Of course, I'll come," she stuttered.)

- **Emotional backdrop:**
  - TELL when a feeling anchors or intensifies the moment. ("He was furious—and not just at her.")
  - SHOW when the emotion builds, leaks, or erupts (clipped speech, heated words, outright aggression).
- **Desire and motivation:**
  - TELL to orient readers inside a character's goal. ("She needed him to believe her, just this once.")
  - SHOW through what the character says, does, and focuses on (fixating on his reaction, pushing too hard, lying).
- **Subtext and repression:**
  - TELL what the character won't express out loud. ("She couldn't say it—not here, not yet.")
  - SHOW the tension in body language, pauses, avoidance, or misdirection.
- **Judgments and perceptions:**
  - TELL internal assessments. ("He looked like someone who got away with everything.")
  - SHOW how they treat the person—dismissive, deferential, combative.
- **Pacing between moments:**
  - TELL to compress or skip the connective tissue. ("They argued for twenty minutes. Then she dropped the bomb.")
  - SHOW the one or two revealing exchanges—the line that turns the fight, the silence that lands like a slap.
- **Setting details:**
  - TELL to orient readers in time of day, temperature, season, basic geography, etc. ("The sun clawed its

way above the horizon, and the alley behind the bar smelled like piss in the harsh daylight.")
- o SHOW when setting interacts with character or action, e.g., rain dripping down his back.
- **Secrets or tension the reader needs in order to understand the moment's gravity:**
  - o TELL what the POV character knows but is hiding. ("She asked it like a question, but she already knew the answer.")
  - o SHOW the act of hiding—polite words with sharp edges, distractions, overcompensation.
- **Inner struggle:**
  - o TELL the contradiction, clearly and with punch. ("She wanted to scream. Instead, she apologized.")
  - o SHOW emotional whiplash—shift in tone, touch, attention, posture.
- **Repeated patterns or history:**
  - o TELL when scene echoes prior behavior. ("It was the same fight they'd had a dozen times, but now, something cracked open.")
  - o SHOW the new variation—what's different, more desperate, more final.
- **Transitions:**
  - o TELL to move through time or space: "By the time they reached the car, she had already made up her mind."
  - o SHOW when something happens during the transition that'll become relevant or lead to a revised plan.
- **Reversals or shifts:**
  - o TELL to mark a beat change. ("She realized, too late, she was the one being played.")
  - o SHOW the cues leading to the reveal landing—new evidence, surprise gestures, chilling silence.

- **Functional info (but not the point)**:
  - TELL setup mechanics. ("He set the glass down and stepped closer.")
  - SHOW when how it's done carries emotional or relational weight, e.g., slamming vs. sliding the glass.

Here's a handy decision tree you can use as you assemble your plot, scene by scene, from the above elements and decide whether to summarize or expand each event into full narrative. The choice is yours. Whenever you're writing, consider the following little decision tree:

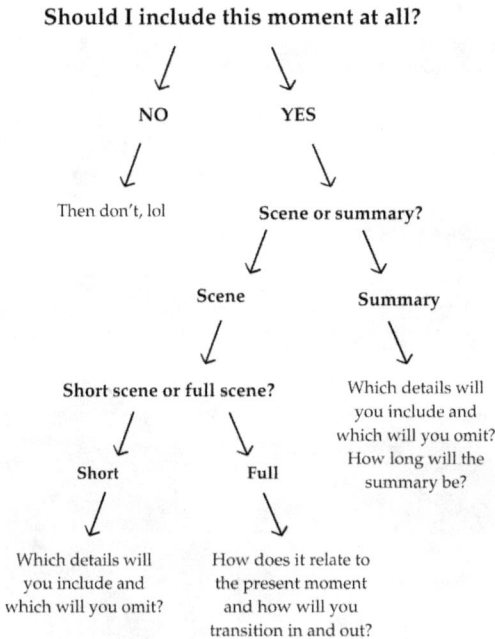

Should I include this moment at all?

NO → Then don't, lol

YES → **Scene or summary?**

Scene → **Short scene or full scene?**

Summary → Which details will you include and which will you omit? How long will the summary be?

Short → Which details will you include and which will you omit?

Full → How does it relate to the present moment and how will you transition in and out?

153

Cut the fluff and get to the good stuff. And if you find that removes about 40% of your manuscript, add more good stuff. Logistical play-by-play and choreography aren't storytelling, I'm afraid. Neither is interiority that floats around in limbo. We have to create a narrative from all of these components, and this involves a lot of decision-making and trial and error. Luckily, that's also where the creative play and excitement can come in.

But first, there's one remaining major writing craft topic left to tackle: a story's world and rules.

10

TELLING ABOUT SETTING AND WORLD

This chapter isn't intended to be a comprehensive guide to world-building, especially for those of you who are writing historical, fantasy, and sci-fi projects (these genres naturally involve more robust story worlds, even if some historical is set in our reality). For speculative writers, I'd strongly suggest *Wonderbook* by Jeff VanderMeer. That said, each story has a specific setting, and each environment should be designed to both challenge and illuminate your protagonist and plot. For example, a story about a rebellious teenager might fall flat until we set it in a dystopian and authoritarian society. Then you'll be adding tons of stakes and potential conflicts for your character to explore as she tests her value system and boundaries.

But our real world has setting considerations, too. No matter the location—domestic or international, rural or urban—the story will involve official/unofficial and spoken/unspoken cultural dynamics, power hierarchies, domestic environments, and social mores. As a result, your characters will have certain worldviews, beliefs, blind spots, prejudices, assumptions, and goals which likely have their genesis in the outside world. Did that rebellious teenager want to excel as a leader on her own steam and for her own reasons? Or is she doing so in part because she perceives her parents' generation as weak and powerless? Is her inner self constantly whispering, "You can't end up like them"? Your protagonist will always be a combination of nature and nurture, and the story world inevitably plays a role in the latter.

Setting can also be extremely powerful in, well, *setting*[1] up your story premise. Here are some elements to consider as you design each location component of your story:

- Where are we? Is this place new, or does it have significance for the protagonist?
- What's the vibe or tone of the setting? What kind of images, sensory details, and descriptions might you use to underscore the vibe of the location?
- What kind of interaction does your protagonist have with the place? Do they feel comfortable there, or are they out of their element?
- When are we in the day? What's the season? The weather?
- Does a familiar setting reappear in a similar or starkly different context later in the story? One of my favorite tricks is tying character arc to place. Who your protagonist is in this environment offers an example of where they are in their development. The next time we visit, they might act, react, feel, or think very differently. (You can also set your final scene in the same spot as your opening to really bring your story and character arc full circle.)

Moving beyond setting, you might want to consider the following world-building elements, which can be rendered in

---

1. Love a good pun. Can't stop, won't stop.

both showing and telling. Most writers treat world-building like set design. What the castle looks like. What year the war happened. How long the skytrain takes to cross the floating archipelago. But it isn't just about describing a place—it's about revealing a protagonist's external context, and how it informs what's going on inside. The real power of world-building comes not from the facts themselves, but from how the characters interpret those facts. Your story world isn't a neutral backdrop. It's an active, value-loaded, and biased system that shapes—and is shaped by—the people in it.

Here's what this means in practice, regardless of the genre you're writing. World-building involves:

- **Character perception**. A crowded apartment means "we're poor" to one narrator, "we're safe" to another, and "we're suffocating" to a third. The world is built through what your characters notice, judge, fear, or long for.
- **Cultural logic**. Rules, rituals, slang, and shared beliefs define a society. Who gets to speak? Who gets left behind? What makes someone important, dangerous, or invisible? Your reader doesn't need a census—they need context.
- **Stakes**. The moment something "normal" is threatened or broken—that's when it matters. Your floating city doesn't become real until it starts to fall. Your court hierarchy doesn't matter until your hero refuses to kneel.
- **Emotions**. If your protagonist's world never chafes, confines, or seduces them, it won't grip your reader either. The best world-building isn't about architecture. It's about friction.

In other words: World-building isn't what your character sees. It's what they believe about what they see—and what this belief means to them (or costs them). So yes, tell us about the coin system or the Great Fungal Uprising, if it matters. But don't get lost in trivia. Build a world your character wants something from—and then don't let them have it without a fight.

Here's how you can apply both telling and showing to world-building elements, no matter your genre:

- **Cultural norms and taboos (what's considered polite, scandalous, shameful):**
  - TELL briefly to orient readers to what's acceptable or shocking in this world.
  - SHOW when a character polices or violates a norm—e.g., gasps at a wedding toast or gets shamed for their appearance or ideas.
- **Geographic or social setting (region, climate, class, urban/rural distinctions):**
  - TELL when giving quick orientation: "The town was split between shit-caked ranchers and crude-covered oil barons."
  - SHOW through sensory detail, local lingo, and character attitudes—e.g., small-town gossip or big-city burnout.
- **Family structures and dynamics (matriarchal, estranged, communal):**
  - TELL to clarify non-normative setups (polyamorous parents, wayward siblings, intergenerational homes).
  - SHOW through interaction, obligation, silence, or conflict at family meals or holidays.
- **Education systems (tracking, standardized testing, prep school culture):**
  - TELL to explain how college acceptances, cafeteria hierarchies, or homeschooling affect daily experiences and social stakes.

- o SHOW with overworked students, school uniforms, detentions, or parent-teacher conflicts.
- **Professional subcultures (restaurant kitchens, hospitals, military, publishing):**
  - o TELL sparingly to create credibility. "In kitchens like this, yelling wasn't cruelty—it was choreography."
  - o SHOW via terminology, tempo, or tension between veterans and outsiders.
- **Historical context (wars, economic shifts, political changes that affect daily life):**
  - o TELL to establish details that affect behavior— e.g., post-Soviet collapse, COVID aftermath, etc.
  - o SHOW artifacts, generational trauma in the present, characters' distorted recollections, or social justice protests.
- **Religion or spiritual practices (rituals, holidays, regional variations):**
  - o TELL when beliefs shape community norms or create tension. ("Most kids in Southie were baptized Catholic by second grade.")
  - o SHOW in rituals, prayer, judgment, conflict over values, or absence of belief.
- **Legal or bureaucratic systems (immigration, custody law, juvenile justice):**
  - o TELL when clarifying stakes—e.g., custody rules, immigration laws, parole violations, etc.
  - o SHOW in obstacles and character strategies (long lines, bribes, court scenes).
- **Healthcare systems and accessibility (especially cross-cultural or historical):**
  - o TELL to clarify socioeconomic disparities or cultural norms. ("Doctors here didn't explain. They prescribed.")

- SHOW through emotional reactions to illness, denial, or medical red tape.
- **Neighborhood dynamics (gentrification, redlining, intergenerational histories):**
  - TELL to quickly sketch a place: "This was a neighborhood where old money strolled the boulevards and new money drove Teslas."
  - SHOW via gossip, storefronts, street encounters, transportation logistics, or code-switching.
- **Technology use and etiquette (smartphones, social media norms):**
  - TELL to note generational or class differences. ("Parents here checked yesterday's grades online before saying 'good morning.'")
  - SHOW via DM drama, ghosting, or "do not disturb" breaches.
- **Gender roles and expectations (especially in a specific time/place):**
  - TELL when contextualizing pressures or norms ("Girls were raised to apologize before speaking.")
  - SHOW through body language, social shaming, double standards, etc.
- **Generational differences in worldview (immigrant parents vs. second-generation kids):**
  - TELL to set the scene. ("To her grandmother, therapy was weakness. To her, it was hygiene.")
  - SHOW in miscommunications, gifts, parenting clashes, or eye-rolls.
- **Class distinctions (what is considered aspirational or embarrassing):**
  - TELL when explaining subtle social cues or unspoken codes. ("Real wealth didn't wear logos.")
  - SHOW through food, lifestyle, housing, transportation, and shame.

- **Local slang or dialects:**
  - TELL for clarity if the usage is heavy or unfamiliar. ("Down here, 'bless your heart' wasn't a compliment.")
  - SHOW in voice and character dynamics—but beware confusing the reader. Also, don't overdo it on the slang or any kind of dialect inflection, as these can easily get overwhelming and overshadow other characterizing elements.
- **Government/political structures (especially in corrupt or authoritarian regimes):**
  - TELL to outline power structures, corruption, or threat levels.
  - SHOW through protest, fear, red tape, propaganda, or silence.

In addition to the above, the following world-building elements tend to be more relevant in fantasy and science fiction stories:

- **Magic systems and limitations (rules, cost, source, who can access it):**
  - TELL to explain rules, cost, access, and consequences (especially early on).
  - SHOW when magic fails, backfires, or takes a toll in unexpected ways.
- **Alternate histories or timelines (what diverged and what changed as a result):**
  - TELL to explain inflection points. ("In 2072, the sun blinked out for a day. Nothing was ever the same again.")
  - SHOW the consequences through tech, fashion, ideology, or fear.
- **Fantastical geography (fae castles, underground kingdoms, multiverses):**

- TELL briefly for orientation. ("The sky road connected the floating cities.")
- SHOW through awe, navigational challenges, or conflict over borders.

- **Species/races and their dynamics (hierarchies, tensions, alliances):**
  - TELL the big picture: who's in power, who's marginalized.
  - SHOW through prejudice, alliances, assimilation, or rebellion.

- **Technology and its integration (implantable tech, AI governance, time travel):**
  - TELL to explain how the tech works or how society has changed as a result of its inception.
  - SHOW its use, misuse, ubiquity—or absence.

- **Religion/mythology unique to the world (pantheons, heresies, prophecies):**
  - TELL when explaining a prophecy, origin story, or ideological schism.
  - SHOW in rituals, fanatics, heretics, or sacred objects.

- **Government systems (matriarchies, technocracies, theocratic empires):**
  - TELL to orient readers to who's in charge and why.
  - SHOW in arrests, surveillance, bureaucratic absurdities, or rebellion.

- **Currency and economy (magic-based, barter, cyber-credits, caste-based labor):**
  - TELL when the currency is unusual or symbolic—e.g., magic ink, memories, etc.
  - SHOW in trades, bartering, black market behavior, or scarcity.

- **Wars or major past events (Great Collapse, Mage War, colonization):**

- TELL through folklore, textbooks, or character backstory.
- SHOW lasting scars: architecture, trauma, landmines, or revenge.
- **Daily life rituals (bonding ceremonies, dream-sharing, self-care):**
  - TELL briefly for context. ("Every home kept a fire burning, for the ancestors.")
  - SHOW how it's performed, enforced, or broken (including the consequences).
- **Social rules/taboos (mind-reading etiquette, purity laws):**
  - TELL to clarify stakes. ("Touching someone's shadow was a proposal, so I made sure to stay out of the sun entirely.")
  - SHOW the fallout from a violation or a near-miss.
- **Language quirks (honorifics, pronoun systems, telepathic communication):**
  - TELL if the terms or rules will confuse the reader.
  - SHOW when meaning is revealed slowly through action or subtext.
- **Time or physics manipulation (loop laws, stasis bubbles, gravity taxes):**
  - TELL to avoid reader confusion: how stasis, time slips, or other mind-bending elements work.
  - SHOW the tension and consequences of these distortions.
- **Interspecies or interplanetary politics (peace treaties, colonial resentment):**
  - TELL for key alliances or historical grudges.
  - SHOW via diplomacy, double-crosses, or inter-species tension.
- **Genetic modification or enhancement norms (e.g., bio-ethics, gene editing):**
  - TELL to clarify norms, laws, or prejudices.

  - ○ SHOW the emotional impact—envy, power, danger.
- **Education/training systems (battle schools, magic academies, training gauntlets):**
  - ○ TELL to explain ranking, eligibility, or lore.
  - ○ SHOW initiation rituals, rivalries, or graduation rites.
- **Transport systems (portals, teleport nets, wormholes with toll booths):**
  - ○ TELL for logistics, e.g., how portals or ships work.
  - ○ SHOW through travel complications, costs, or quests.
- **World-ending threats (explained mythically or scientifically):**
  - ○ TELL for backstory. ("The sky beasts came once before. We barely survived.")
  - ○ SHOW current tension, preparation, denial, or awe.

Without further ado, here are examples of telling used to support world-building and setting from the shelves, starting with contemporary realistic (non-speculative) stories.

Contemporary Realistic World-building

Let's kick off with some setting description of an indigenous reservation from *Rez Ball* by Byron Graves. Our protagonist, Tre, makes sure to introduce the place he lives—the "rez"— because some people don't have the direct experience or knowledge of such a culturally specific place. And besides, reservations aren't a monolith. This character comes from the Ojibwe tribe, which has its own social mores, rules, and traditions. We get this flyover early on:

That's kind of how our rez is. A mix of rugged and

pretty. Ten minutes of driving through the rez and we pass by the casino that sits right on the rez line. After that it's a half hour ride through dense forest, then flat farmland and past smelly cows as we get closer to the city of Bemidji.[i]

But not all setting description is quite so literal. As we saw at the beginning of this chapter, there is a lot more to world-building than a story's physical surroundings.

We can also establish family history and cultural issues. The next excerpt, from the thriller *The House Across the Lake* by Riley Sager, is another take on land that was once indigenous, but the below takes a different angle and summarizes the chain of ownership:

> The lake house has always been a special place for my family. Conceived by my great-great-grandfather as an escape from New York's steaming, stinking summers, it was once the only residence on this unassuming splash of water. That's how the lake got its name. Originally called Lake Otshee by the indigenous tribe that once lived in the area, it was renamed Lake Greene in honor of the first white man intrepid enough to build here because, well, America.[ii]

Instead of simply describing the place, the author offers some history, (colorful) description, and social commentary about the lake being renamed and American colonialist attitudes.[2] Readers also learn about the protagonist's ancestors and ties to the location, which is very important to this specific novel, as you can tell from its title.

---

2. One could argue that Casey, a white woman, is in a privileged position to own multiple homes, enjoys generational wealth, and shouldn't be joking about these issues.

CHAPTER 10

World-building telling can also provide cultural context for an institution. The following excerpt, from *Tomorrow, and Tomorrow, and Tomorrow* by Gabrielle Zevin, introduces audiences to an outsider's perspective of MIT:

> Sadie sometimes felt as if she could go weeks without seeing a woman. It might have been that the men, most of them at least, assumed you were stupid if you were a woman. Or, if not stupid, less smart than they were. They were operating under the assumption that it was easier to get into MIT if you were a woman, and statistically, it was—women had a 10 percent higher admittance rate over men. But there could have been many reasons for that statistic. A likely one was self-elimination: female applicants to MIT might have held themselves to higher standards than male applicants. The conclusion should not have been that the women who got into MIT were less gifted, less worthy of their places, and yet, that seemed to be what it was.[iii]

This passage offers a description of what's currently happening at the university but also includes some commentary about the dearth of female students and what it suggests to the men who overwhelmingly dominate the institution's demographics. Not only are women underrepresented (officially), but they're disparaged (unofficially), which is very relevant to this particular story and our female protagonist, Sadie.

Occupations have cultures as well. This publishing industry world-building from *Yellowface* by R.F. Kuang is inflected by the POV protagonist, June's, position as a self-identified outsider, which adds some emotion and tension:

> Publishing picks a winner—someone attractive

enough, someone cool and young and, oh, we're all thinking it, let's just say it, "diverse" enough—and lavishes all its money and resources on them.[iv]

This description isn't inaccurate, but the bitter tone comes from June feeling entitled to those resources and not getting them. There's also some larger social and cultural commentary about performative diversity and inclusion initiatives, which peg this novel in an American cultural moment in time.

An intersection of world-building and worldview comes from the upmarket novel *All Fours* by Miranda July, in which an unnamed protagonist unpacks contemporary sexism and double standards for female and male parents on either side of welcoming a child. Her husband, Harris, does very little (according to her biased viewpoint) but gets rewarded, whereas she feels judged and shamed:

> Without a child I could dance across the sexism of my era, whereas becoming a mother shoved my face right down into it. A latent bias, internalized by both of us, suddenly leapt forth in parenthood. It was now obvious that Harris was openly rewarded for each thing he did while I was quietly shamed for the same things. There was no way to fight back against this, no one to point a finger at, because it came from everywhere.[v]

The image of "it came from everywhere" as it pertains to these attitudes is especially relevant to her culture. But, of course, this is a perspective specific to a put-upon mother character. Harris might think about his transition into fatherhood very differently, which reminds us that setting, world, social, and cultural assessments are informed by a character's specific lived experience, station, and life stage.

CHAPTER 10

The next excerpt tackles a Filipino cultural expectation, that of being indebted to one's ancestors, from the YA novel *Everything We Never Had* by Randy Ribay. This beautiful story weaves together multiple POV narrators and timelines and charts members of the same immigrant family across time. Here's how the first-generation character, Enzo, explains the idea of *"utang na loob."* The jumping-off point for this instance of telling is a conversation with another Filipino character, Chris. However, this section is mostly for the reader's benefit, working to set the tone and offer context. The author and publisher likely felt this custom needed some additional telling:

> *Utang na loob*: a debt from within. From the heart. It is a debt you did not ask for and will never pay off but must always try to. It is gratitude for the ancestors who brought you into existence, for the family who raised you, for the community who helped you in ways direct and indirect, visible and invisible. It is acknowledgment that none of us are alone.
>
> For those who left, it is remittances. It is balikbayan boxes. It is donations for every typhoon, every eruption. It is massive multilingual family group chats. It is saying yes to being ninong or ninang to children you've never met. It is flying across the world for weddings and funerals and worrying about the savings account or credit cards later. It is the shame of missing weddings and funerals because the savings account is empty and the credit cards have reached their limit.
>
> It is beautiful. It is burdensome.
>
> It is the glue of community, the weight of obligation.
>
> Chris also sighs. Nods. "Utang na loob."[vi]

To keep this from being a dry and academic explanation, notice how Enzo explores his feelings about this obligation, and how some truly lovely and insightful writing accompanies the telling. By using a specific voice and shooting the information through a character's lens, the author is able to avoid making this information burdensome.

Historical projects, especially, need to do a lot of world-building. Not just for scene-setting and to establish period details, but for cultural information as well. For example, nobody alive today has the experience of being an enslaved person during the peak of the Transatlantic slave trade. However, the finer cultural points come alive in *James* by Percival Everett, as Jim goes about his business as a Black man at the very bottom of society (I originally discussed Jim's masking through dialogue and dialect in Chapter 3.) This is demonstrated here, as Jim and another Black man laugh, only to slip back into character when a white man comes along:

> We started to laugh and then we spotted a white man up the road. There was nothing that irritated white men more than a couple of slaves laughing. I suspected they were afraid we were laughing at them or else they simply hated the idea of us having a good time. Whatever the case, we were slow to hush and so captured his attention. He'd heard us and walked our way.[vii]

"There was nothing that irritated white men more than a couple of slaves laughing" is likely hard-won wisdom. When paired with the idea of how little a Black life meant at that time, the potential stakes of breaking this social expectation would be astronomical. A seemingly small moment—even a lighthearted one—could turn deadly. While the rule is explained rather explicitly here, what's merely implied and shown is the constant vigilance of being Black during this period. Jim can't even laugh without looking over his shoulder. And *that's* world-building, too. Not just the rule, but its ramifications as they affect a character's behavior.

Now let's pivot to how speculative world-building is built using a combination of telling and showing.

Speculative World-building

There tend to be more rules and world-building details in fantasy and science-fiction. In many cases, writers in these genres have made their ideas up from whole cloth. Sometimes a lot of explanation is necessary because we don't have reverse gravity and oxygen rationing in our world (yet!), and readers have no pre-existing framework for understanding these elements. The main obstacle in transmitting this amount of setting data is avoiding the dreaded info-dump. *Especially* at the beginning of the story, where a writer might be *most* tempted to explain everything.

So on the one hand, we have a lot of information to transmit. On the other, we must launch into scene and character with enough pacing to get the narrative off the ground and hook readers. These two ideas are in an uneasy balance of action and information. (Or maybe even ... showing ... *and* ... telling?[3])

The advice I always give, and explore in more depth in *Writing Irresistible First Pages*, is to offer readers only as much information at the very beginning of a narrative as necessary to ensure the world and conflict make sense to outside readers, then backfill more later. But this can be a difficult needle to thread for fantasy, sci-fi, and historical. Let's see how some published examples do it.

---

3. Before you ask, yes, I am, indeed, very pleased with myself for this one.

Our first excerpt comes from *What the River Knows* by Isabel Ibañez, a YA historical mystery with a speculative element. If you pick this one up and read the first chapter, you will notice there's a lot of information delivered about a number of story pillars: the cultural context (our character, Inez, has spent her life living in Argentina with her uncle); the historical period (especially as it pertains to expectations for young women); backstory about Inez's missing parents (who disappeared on an archaeological trip to Egypt and are presumed dead); and, of course, the fantasy logistics of the world (predicated on objects with magical signatures, which our protagonist just so happens to be able to sense). It's a tall order to get all of the above on the page expediently and without tanking the pacing:

> Papá once explained it to me like this: long ago, before people built their cities, before they decided to root themselves to one area, past generations of Spellcasters from all around the world created magic with rare plants and hard-to-find ingredients. With every spell performed, the magic gave up a spark, an otherworldly energy that was quite literally heavy. As a result, it would latch on to surrounding objects, leaving behind an imprint of the spell. A natural byproduct of performing magic. [viii]

This story has a nature-based magic system, where spells originate from organic ingredients and generate energy, which latches on to objects. These are the items Inez will track across the world to solve the mystery of her parents' disappearance, so it's crucial information to install in reader imaginations early on. Notice that the author doesn't spend much time dressing this information up or trying to show it. We get "Papá once explained," followed by the explanation. It's important to note that historical, sci-fi, and fantasy readers tend to be a bit more tolerant of exposition and world-building data, simply because they're used to this genre convention. You could really waste a lot of your precious creative writing energy trying to show this stuff. Or you can play within established genre and audience expectations and indulge in some telling (as long as you don't go fully overboard, of course).

The following is an expression of a character's powers, this time from the YA fantasy novel *Heir* by Sabaa Tahir. I wanted to juxtapose this with the previous world-building example because the magic is similar, but each author has taken it in a slightly different direction:

> Her magic lived in her blood. Had since birth. It was as steady as breathing or having skin. Or it had been, until now.
>
> Sirsha walked farther down the hillside, leaving the horse her client had given her to graze on the sparse winter grasses. She put her hand to the earth. Nothing. A thousand threads, a thousand trails—none of which mattered. The wind spun dead leaves around her, swirled dust into her eyes.
>
> "If you're not going to help"—Sirsha coughed and battered the dust away—"then piss off."
>
> A low, sullen hiss. *Follow the bones.*
>
> She scanned the scrubby land, which was filled with ravines and gulches. The wind's hints were never idle. If the bones weren't near, it wouldn't have said anything. She walked across the dead, snow-dusted grass to a spot that dropped away into a gully. There, at the bottom, she saw a flash of dull white.[ix]

Here, we combine action with magical explanation. The character, Sirsha, is on the outside of society, an exiled mercenary, trying to track a killer who has been targeting children. We see what her innate magic feels like when she interfaces with it during an active hunt for clues. Not only are we treated to some nice scene-setting about the environment, but we see secondhand (since this is third person) that Sirsha's magic speaks to her via the wind. There's even some humor. She wants the wind to guide her, not blow dust in her face, and talks to it like it's an annoying sibling.

Then we're shown how the magic conveys information to her and told "the wind's hints were never idle." That's an example of a hard-and-fast magical rule. From this point on, readers will trust the wind's whispers. If the wind *does* happen to lie or misdirect Sirsha, this change to the established rules will have to be addressed in order for the magic to have consistent logic and, more importantly, boundaries. Boundless magic is actually quite boring because readers will never truly worry for a protagonist who wields it. They can get out of any conflict and, as a result, the story loses its crucial ability to create and raise stakes.

The next excerpt is from the historical (and modern) multi-timeline, multi-POV *Bury Our Bones in the Midnight Soil* by V.E. Schwab. María, who we first met in Chapter 5, has accidentally and suddenly been changed into a vampire, but this event also kills her maker, so she has absolutely no idea what the vampire rules are. This is perhaps a contrivance so she can meet some more established (and knowledgeable) vampires and learn the paranormal parameters of her world, at least as far as this author has molded them:

"Are there other ways to die?" she asks, thinking of the widow, crumbling to ash against her dress.
"Yes, and no," says Renata. "Your bones will set. Your skin will mend. But the heart alone stays mortal. It is the seat of life, and death. If it is ruined, or removed, severed from the head or drained of all its

blood, there is no mending to be done. When the heart collapses, so do we. If you must die," she adds thoughtfully, "a blade or stick is quick, a bite is kind, but fire is a bad end."[x]

Renata, an older vampire who's seen more ways their kind can get hurt and die, goes on to explain that in a fire, the heart burns last from its rather insulated place in the chest cavity, meaning a burning vampire will be alive and in pain until the last possible moment. This conversation is telling, framed as a cautionary tale.[4] In this specific case, you might be wondering why any explanation is needed at all. Everyone knows vampire lore by this point in history, right?[5] Well, not quite. And there's absolutely no rule that says you can't innovate on existing canonical ideas for popular magical creatures or invent some of your own. In fact, I encourage you to think freely about your world-building.

The following witch story, *The Invocations* by Krystal Sutherland, creates a unique magic system of "invocation" magic, which gives women powers when they bind a piece of their souls to a demon. A special type of witch must "write" the spell and oversee the process. However, some characters, like Jude, who we met in Chapter 4, go to the dark side, binding invocations to themselves, giving up too much of their souls, and otherwise breaking the rules. But wait, there's more! Someone else—a man, they suspect—is murdering women for their invocations, which are seared into their skin. Here's how an anonymous POV, who's being stalked in the night, explains some of the rules in the prologue:

---

4. Spoiler alert: It's also Chekov's gun and foreshadows exactly how a vampire will die in the story.
5. I'd argue this is a fallacy since different cultures have different versions of these stories.

It is impossible. Men cannot use magic. This is what she has been told. This is what she has been promised. Men cannot write spells. Men cannot sear invocations into their skin. Men cannot bind their souls to demons in exchange for power.[xi]

This statement of world-building fact comes up because the character observes her pursuer using power normally reserved for women. Her explanation, which is telling, is in reaction to something going *wrong* with the magical world as she knows it. It's almost as if she's reminding *herself* of the rules once she sees them broken. This also serves to transmit information to readers. You, too, can take this paradoxical approach: "This is how the world has always worked. So what's wrong now?"

Next up are two excerpts from *The Fox Wife* by Yangsze Choo, a historical fantasy featuring immortal fox spirits. Here's how Snow explains not only the difference between fox spirits and ghosts, but the culturally specific idea of *yin* and *qi*, which reflects the Manchurian and Japanese setting of the story (there's also a little bit of sass, which adds voice):

Ghosts and foxes, though often confused by people, are quite different. For one thing, ghosts belong to the world of the dead and are therefore *yin*, or negative energy. Some people think foxes are similar because we go around collecting *qi*, or life force, but nothing could be further from the truth. We are living creatures, just like you, only usually better-looking.[xii]

Whereas the narrator of *What the River Knows*, Inez, took a "Papá explained" approach, Snow uses another common gambit: "Most people think X, but I'm here to tell you that it's *really* Y." By invoking what she claims is a misconception, she indulges in some telling to set the record straight. The former frame is very straightforward and doesn't try to disguise the telling at all. The latter version is a little more sly, even though the text on the page is still an explanation. Whether you're obvious with your world-building or you dress it up with a little flair is up to you.

The same novel offers another frame for telling on the topic of boundaries around fox immortality:

> A fox who lives for more than a hundred years will be tested with catastrophe. Some say that is heaven's way of eliminating creatures who live too long. At one hundred years of age, it's said, lightning strikes from heaven. At two hundred, an earthquake will try to swallow you. At three hundred, a raging ball of fire appears. Naturally, foxes who die have never passed on the exact details. All we know is that we will each face trials; if you can survive for a thousand years, you may reach enlightenment.
> Or so they say.[xiii]

Here, readers also learn about the spiritual component to an unnaturally long life, and discover enlightenment might be possible for a select few. (It's implied that Snow might want it.) But all of this explanation is wrapped up in the folksy narrative gambit of "some say" and "or so they say." Snow is passing on gossip and acting as a co-conspirator with the reader. This can create a frisson of excitement as audiences are let in on a secret, which may also distract them from what is, in fact, just telling.

Our last example comes from fan favorite romantasy *The Fourth Wing* by Rebecca Yarros. Violet is all set to be a scribe in a society which prizes might and dragon power over knowledge and softness. Unfortunately, her mother is the general of their army, and orders Violet to take part in dangerous trials to potentially bond with a dragon … if she survives. Mira is her protective older sister. Here, we see the family discussing their backstory, a demonstration of Mom's dragon magic, and some world history as well:

> "Are you that eager to bury another child?" Mira seethes.
> I cringe as the temperature in the room plummets, courtesy of Mom's storm-wielding signet power she channels through her dragon, Aimsir. My chest tightens at the memory of my brother. No one has dared to mention Brennan or his dragon in the five years since they died fighting the Tyrrish rebellion in the south. Mom tolerates me and respects Mira, but she loved Brennan.[xiv]

While this moment comes from a scene with multiple characters in action, it's mostly information. Mira's dialogue is expository. We learn about the older brother, Brennan's, death here, too. Mom reacts badly, with a little help from her dragon and "storm-wielding signet power," which readers are still learning about. In interiority, Violet adds more context to the tragedy, while also dropping some logistical place names and details which bolster the audience's knowledge of this world's ongoing war. Instead of dramatizing past grief, she tells us how it lingers. It's efficient and emotionally truthful.

We could have done a flashback to the moment the family learned of Brennan's death, with Mom dropping to her knees and wailing, etc., but why? Readers get all they need from this summary, including outright telling about Mom's relationship to each of her children: she apparently "tolerates" Violet, "respects" Mira, but saved all her love for Brennan. This passage is basically all telling, except for the opening line of dialogue—but even *that* contains, you guessed it, telling!

Implicit throughout are the stakes: Brennan has actually died. This is real. Death has visited their doorstep, despite Mom's high status. If Violet goes through with the trials, there is a very real chance she'll become Mom's next dead child. But in addition to these ideas, which readers must interpret from the text, there is also a lot of explanation.

My honest hope is that you'll start to notice telling in the books you're reading, examine why and how it's used, and decide which strategies make sense for your own writing. Our final chapter will use a Q&A format to suggest redirects and strategies for addressing common showing and telling issues you might encounter in your work.

11

COMMON SHOWING AND TELLING CRAFT QUESTIONS (AND ANSWERS!)

Now you've read this guide. You've nodded sagely. You've highlighted things and muttered "okay, yeah, that makes sense" under your breath. (Or so I hope!) But you might then go back to your own work and immediately think:

- *But this still feels flat.*
- *But my critique group didn't connect with it.*
- *But now my voice sounds dead.*

Welcome to the craft panic spiral. It can sweep perfectly capable writers into a frenzy once they've internalized writing advice but don't yet know how to apply it to their own scenes without destabilizing the stuff that's already working.

The good news is, most of the problems you're seeing in your work—or hearing about in feedback—are not mysterious. They're just misfires. A beat told when it should've been shown, or vice versa. A moment underwritten. A sentence which presents information three times in a row just to be safe. You're not messing it up or missing the point. You're learning how to use a whole new toolkit. This is where we sharpen it.

Q: In an effort to follow "show, don't tell" to the letter, I find my writing is full of physical clichés. How do I correct for this?

This is perhaps the biggest trap writers fall into when they wholeheartedly commit to the "show, don't tell" advice. They believe they must only touch upon emotion that can be perceived or expressed using the physical body, so we get "her heart hammered in her throat," "his cheeks flushed with rage," and "she balled her fists at her sides." But think of these as a collection of external symptoms only. In medicine, what can be observed during an exam is just one part of an underlying diagnosis. The truth is, any number of thoughts or feelings can lead to a character physically expressing frustration. What if she balls her hands at her sides in determination after scoring the winning basket? That won't make sense unless we know she was trying to beat her previous vertical record. And we can only know that if she (or a narrator) tells us. **Instead of rendering the physical reaction on the page, go back one step to the interiority**: *If only she hadn't skipped leg day this week, she would've made it*. Or: *I didn't want to hear them clapping. It wasn't my best, and that's nothing to celebrate*. You can then add some clenched fists for good measure, but if that's *all* you're providing, you will remain at a superficial level in your writing until you break yourself of this habit.

Q: What if readers find it tough to connect to my *character*?

My guess is you're under-explaining motivation, need, or stakes. *Why* something matters is invariably more important than the thing itself. The external stimulus could be as life-changing as a marriage proposal or as seemingly inconsequential as a slip of paper with a temporary tattoo on it. You might not need to explain why a proposal is a big deal (though your story should do a good job of showing *and* telling whether the two characters involved are suited for marriage). But you might need to add a bit of context for the temporary tattoo. Maybe it's the last thing a young protagonist's friend gave her during a magical-seeming summer before moving away with his family. Sure, it's "just" a piece of paper, but if you do the work to imbue it with meaning, it can become so much more. High emotional resonance for characters and readers isn't only found in the life-changing moments. Those will seem hollow if you haven't done the work to create the ecosystem of your character's values, desires, needs, and previous deeply felt reactions to events both big and small. Readers need to know a character's emotional landscape and how they make meaning from the set pieces of their lives, too. If you realize *you* don't know—start there.

Q: What if readers struggle to connect to the *emotion* in my work?

Emotionless voice usually comes from pure showing and under-telling. The scene is technically clear—characters move, speak, emote—but it reads as sterile, emotionally distant, or generic. This happens when a writer is trying so hard to "show, don't tell" that they've stripped out the narrative lens —there's no internal commentary, filter, or character POV embedded in the prose. It's a GoPro mounted to a tripod, not a narrator with a pulse. To address this, inject interiority and filtered observation. Let the POV character interpret the scene and its potential ramifications, not just describe the proceedings. Add a subjective reaction, judgment, or emotional beat. Use voice-infused language choices, too. "He slithered in like a smug little bastard" hits differently than, "He walked into the room." Here's another example of pure showing:

> He set the mug down. "I didn't mean it," he said.
> She crossed her arms. "You never do."

Here's a revision using interiority:

> He set the mug down. "I didn't mean it," he said.
> She crossed her arms. If this was a peace offering,
> it was too little, too late. Of course he didn't *mean it*.
> That was the whole problem.

See the difference? It's the same moment, but now it breathes. If the scene works on paper but not in your gut, check the lens. You might be "showing" like a screenwriter, when what the reader needs is access to how the moment feels.

Consider telling us what the character is thinking, feeling, fearing, justifying, regretting, and wanting. Not all the time. But at key moments, especially when:

- Something changes;
- Something hurts;
- A choice is made; and/or
- A truth is revealed.

Telling here doesn't flatten the story—it juices emotion from what you've already put into motion. If the reader isn't connecting, you're not under-writing. You're under-revealing. And nine times out of ten, that means you're under-telling.

Q: What if I'm getting a lot of notes about my writing being redundant?

My guess is you're using too much telling, which, despite my thesis for this guide, does happen and can overwhelm your writing. Let's break this issue open, too. Sometimes writers layer the same beat three different ways without adding meaning. And yes, excessive telling—especially after the scene already shows the action and emotion—kills pacing, tension, and trust. This isn't usually a plot issue. It's a sentence-level storytelling issue. It usually means you're explaining what the scene already showed.

I understand the urge. You're trying to make sure the reader gets it, so after a line of dialogue, a statement of context, or an action, you restate the emotion and re-explain the motive. This often comes from fear that readers will miss the point. But the effect on audiences is the opposite of what you want. Instead of demonstrating mastery, repetition makes your writing feel insecure.

Instead, cut the echo and keep the strongest beat. Ask yourself:

- Did I already show this?
- Did the action or dialogue imply it?
- Is the emotion legible?
- Am I telling something new, or just restating data?

If the telling adds clarity, contrast, or an unexpected characterizing twist—keep it. This also applies if the context matters to a specific character at this specific moment. If you're just repeating the same information readers have already been shown, told, or both—cut it.

Here's an example of a redundant passage:

"I said I'm fine," she snapped.

She was obviously angry, clearly far from okay.

The following revision is tighter, and all you really need:

"I said I'm *fine*."

Don't worry, we already feel the tension because she's emphasizing "fine" and hitting the "I said," which suggests she knows she's not being very convincing. The second line in the original text just flattens the whole thing. Redundancy is telling which arrives after the scene already did the work. When in doubt, trust the reader. Say it once. Say it well. Then move on.

Q: What if I'm worried telling will strip my writing of its unique voice?

A: This depends on your narrative distance. If you have trouble telling as your POV character, lean into how *they'd* talk about something. You don't need to float about the action as a removed, distant, omniscient narrator in order to add context. People exchange information all day, every day, from their own perspectives. You tell your best friend why the breakup was such a gut-punch. You add context to a project update at work. Voice lives inside telling. You just have to do it on purpose.

You've worked hard to craft a compelling narrative voice. It's sharp, or lyrical, or wry, or biting. And now this guide is urging you to tell more—but every time you do, it feels clunky, like you're hitting pause on the narrative to explain something in a totally different tone.

So you hold back. And the voice stays clear. But it also risks wearing your story emotionally thin.

You're thinking of telling as neutral exposition—like someone stepping out from behind the curtain to give a PowerPoint presentation. That's how most writers were taught to imagine the process of telling. But that's not what I mean by "good telling." Good telling is voiced. It's character-infused. It's alive. It sounds like someone thinking, ranting, regretting, spiraling, rationalizing, etc.

So instead, tell it in your voice. Tell in *your character's* voice. Don't switch gears when you shift into telling. Instead of:

> She had always struggled with control. It was her fatal flaw.

Try it like this:

> Control had always been her thing. Even her playlists were in alphabetical order. That's why she kept her Spotify private.

Readers get the same information. But one version sounds like a distant narrator explaining. The other sounds like a person sharing. Don't be afraid to create writing and telling that reveals bias or interrupts a moment to add commentary —that's voice. Let your syntax flex: sentence fragments, run-ons, rhetorical questions, sarcasm, etc. … it's all fair game. Treat telling like a dialogue with the reader. It's pulling your audience aside, not breaking the story. So don't sterilize it. Stylize it.

Q: What should I do about a skyrocketing word count when I show more scenes?

First, let's acknowledge this problem, which we originally broached in Chapter 8: **scenes are expensive.** Every time you decide to dramatize a moment, you're expending space and time. And if you start "showing" everything, your draft can easily balloon into something bloated, exhausting, and structurally unsound. So what do you do?

- **Get selective.** Not every beat deserves the full cinematic treatment. Save scenes for moments of change, escalation, or emotional heat. If nothing's shifting—internally or externally—it's probably better as summary.
- **Use telling as compression, too.** Telling isn't a cop-out; it's a tool for controlling momentum. Use it to skip the boring stuff, condense connective tissue, and *bridge* the emotional beats between scenes. (That travel montage? That three-week training sequence? Tell it.)
- **Reframe "more scenes" as "sharper storytelling."** More scenes ≠ better story. Intentional, well-placed, and meaningful scenes do more work than a dozen meandering ones.

You don't need fewer scenes—you need **fewer indulgent ones.** Show when it matters. Tell when it doesn't.[1] And don't be afraid to *cut mercilessly* once you've seen what the story actually needs.

Q: Conversely, now that I'm telling more, my story isn't long enough. How do I fix this?

Ah, yes—the "now my story's too short" panic. If you're now looking at a novella after trimming your novel's scenes and summarizing for pace, here's what might've happened.

---

1. Or it doesn't matter … *as much*. If it truly doesn't matter, get rid of it altogether.

- **You summarized away the substance.** Telling is great mortar—but it can't carry the emotional or structural weight of your novel on its own. If you've over-corrected, you've likely stripped the story of scene-level engagement, character depth, and turning points.
- **You left out the tension.** Often, short drafts skip over the hardest, messiest stuff: the conflict, turning points, and emotional contradictions. These are the chewy middle bits that make a story *feel* full. Ask yourself: Where are the moments of *friction*? Do they exist? Or did you summarize them into a tasteful paragraph?
- **You need to go deeper, not wider.** This isn't about adding more plot twists, side quests, or "just one more character." It's about **amplifying the scenes you already have** and adding emotional complexity, interiority, and escalation. Layer it, don't pad it.
- **Work to enrich, not just inflate.** Word count is only a problem if you're measuring value by page numbers. Instead, make sure every page you *do* have carries weight.

If your draft is too short, the answer isn't more filler. It's more fuel. Tell strategically—but don't skip the good stuff.

Q: How do I know if my balance of showing and telling works?

Here's the real talk: **if your reader is fully immersed, you nailed it.** If they're confused, bored, emotionally detached, or stuck in a fog of exposition ... you didn't.

Here's how to consider both sides:

- **Good telling builds trust. Good showing builds presence.** If your telling provides clarity, context, or emotional insight, while avoiding the trap of sounding like a Wikipedia summary, you're off to a great start. If your showing makes readers feel like they're *in it* with the character instead of watching from the nosebleeds, you're golden.

- **Are you moving the story *and* the character?** A healthy balance means you're not just staging cool visuals or explaining motives—you're doing both. You're making audiences care *while* things happen. If all your scenes are dramatic reenactments with no interior lens, or if all your paragraphs are reflective monologues with no forward motion, it's time to recalibrate.

- **Watch your pacing.** Too much showing, and your story can drag under the weight of Real-Time Everything. Too much telling, and your story feels like a summary that leaves readers yawning. If readers are skimming or zoning out, they're pointing out where the imbalance is.

- **Test it out loud (or with a reader).** If *you* feel itchy reading a section—like you're trying too hard, or like nothing's landing—it probably needs a shift. Better yet, ask a trusted reader where they felt most engaged or most disconnected. Their answers will tell you exactly where your ratio is off.

If your story reads smoothly, clearly, and like it's emotionally alive, you've got the balance. If it reads like a bullet-point recap or a movie set frozen between takes … keep playing with it.

Q: How do genre expectations play into the balance of showing and telling?

Genre is your unspoken contract with the reader. Whether they realize it or not, they're walking in with certain expectations around how immersive, introspective, or information-rich the story will be—and how much work they'll have to do to engage with it.

Genre absolutely affects your balance of showing and telling. And ignoring that will make your book feel "off," even if your prose and storytelling beats are technically solid.

Let's break it down:

- **In Thriller, Horror, and Action-Driven Speculative Fiction:**
  - Show the beats. Tell the stakes. Readers want to feel the tension in real time—but they also want clarity. Smart, selective telling helps you compress downtime and keep the plot racing forward. Long internal monologues or dreamy reflection? Trim it.
    - TELL to control pacing.
    - SHOW to heighten immediacy and fear.
- **In Romance, Literary Fiction, and Character-Driven YA or Adult Fiction:**
  - Show the emotion. Tell the insight. These genres thrive on nuance. Readers expect a close interior lens and emotional complexity. That doesn't mean overwriting every heartbeat—but it does mean delivering both texture *and* clarity.
    - TELL to dramatize decisions, transformations, and specific chemistry and connection points.
    - SHOW to decode meaning, relationship dynamics, or the consequences of the above decisions.

- **In Fantasy and Science Fiction (especially epic or secondary world):**
  - Tell the world. Show the impact. Your reader needs to understand the setting, rules, and stakes —quickly. But nobody wants a Wikipedia dump. Smart telling (sprinkled in, not vomited all over the place) can establish context. Showing then demonstrates how the world shapes the character.
    - TELL for orientation and exposition.
    - SHOW to bring unfamiliar worlds to life on a sensory level.
- **In Memoir and Narrative Nonfiction:**
  - Tell the truth. Show the cost. Memoir relies heavily on voice and reflection (telling via interiority), but the moments that land emotionally are almost always dramatized. Readers need to *see* the key scenes play out—then hear what they meant.
    - TELL to shape memory, context, or realization.
    - SHOW to relive the experience and invite readers in.

Genre doesn't dictate how much showing or telling you do— but it *does* impact what your readers will tolerate, expect, or crave. Use that to your advantage.

Q: Is there a "right way" to write or revise?

No! This is the great thing about any creative endeavor. There are multiple ways to address any problem, especially if you agree it's a problem. That's right, you don't need to jump all over each piece of feedback you receive. As long as you're able to be open-minded and can confidently say you're not you're having a knee-jerk defensive reaction, you can pick and choose what you tackle.

You can also decide *how* you'll revise any real or perceived issue that you (or a critique partner, agent, or freelance editor) identifies in your work.

For example, pacing, which was mentioned a few questions above, is one of those nebulous craft concepts that tends to stymie a lot of writers. It's pretty easy for a reader to pick up on slow or quick pacing in storytelling, but writers don't have direct control over the audience's perception and might not know with levers to pull or their ultimate effects.

If you get the note that your pacing is off, how will you address it? There is no one *right* way, especially since every story, genre, target audience, and writer is different, too. How you'd fix pacing in a mystery, thriller, horror, or suspense story is not how you might deal with it (or neglect it entirely) in a serious literary novel.

The below are all valid pacing fixed. Sometimes you'll take one approach, sometimes a combination is the ticket:

- Deleting superfluous backstory;
- Adding dialogue and action;
- Shaving down scene-setting and world information;
- Summarizing transitions instead of dramatizing them;
- Putting entire scenes in compressed narration;
- Using fewer images in your descriptive writing;
- Interspacing informational paragraphs with dialogue and scene; and
- Adding energy to the voice so readers feel the telling sequences are more engaging.

What works for you in one project might not be the solution in another, even if you're the same writer. What works for your critique partner might be terrible advice for *you*.

If there's only one thing you take away from this guide, it's that writing advice isn't one-size-fits-all, nor is it always unquestionably helpful. Take "show, don't tell." Now that we've peeled back the layers and examined the pros and cons of this old chestnut, you might have a deeper understanding of your craft. One that's impossible to summarize in three words.

And that's where the gold is. A more nuanced grasp of yourself as a writer, your toolbox, and the strategies that make sense to you. Sure, it might no longer fit on a bumper sticker or neatly in a Track Changes comment bubble, but it's *your* insight, applicable to *your* work.

CONCLUSION

Whether you love or hate the premise of this guide, I hope the ideas within it inspire you to make your own creative decisions. It's amazing how often I've heard some variant of the following from editorial clients over the years:

> "I know it's not your job, but I feel like you've given me permission."

Whether it's permission to pursue the niche or quirky idea that they've kept on their personal back burner forever, finally write a taboo personal essay regardless of what someone in their life might think, or go back to writing twenty-five years after an English teacher or unsupportive parent or partner told them they'd never amount to anything.

To be clear, as long as you're not engaging in illegal or morally bankrupt activity, nobody needs anyone's permission to do a *damn* thing. But in practice, the idea of permission is much less straightforward. Due to a number of factors (some nature, mostly nurture), creatives feel they can't simply be themselves. Writing is too selfish, too impractical. Their inner critic is always watching and whispering its poisonous insults. There's no time for anything, let alone something as frivolous as scribbling made-up stories as the world burns.[1]

So over and over in my editorial practice, I find myself in the position of offering a mindset shift: Actually, you *can* do it. And you probably *should*, because there's a reason this idea still has its hooks in you, begging to be written, no matter how long you've ignored or avoided it.

As long as your intentions are pure, fucking do it. Go with your gut. Write the thing. The piece may not go on to be published, as there are no guarantees in this tough and competitive industry, but there *is* something soul-fulfilling about getting those words, thoughts, and ideas down on paper or screen.[2]

It's entirely untrue that a writer *needs* my permission to write or challenge yourself, but many feel they *want* it, even if they can't articulate this desire until after we have an eye-opening conversation about their work and creative goals.

In the same exact vein, you don't need my permission to take a long, hard, and unflinching look at the "show, don't tell" advice. For the same reason many people are scared to write —or to write what they most deeply ache to—writers clutch this wisdom like it's sacred.

I get why. But I am also a stubborn asshole who never takes a piece of advice without examining it from all sides.[3] And

---

1. This is actually exactly why we *need* stories now more than ever.
2. All this said, there are some foundational publishing industry guidelines, especially in children's books. The latter are specific to how kids learn to listen to and, later, read stories themselves from a developmental perspective. I can confidently say that you will *never* traditionally publish a 100,000-word picture book. But once we get beyond some of these common-sense rules, let your powerful writing intuition be your guide.
3. I argued so much growing up that my mother always told me I'd be an excellent lawyer, which misunderstands both my personality and the legal profession, but that's a story for another day.

while it *should* go without saying that you must take the wisdom and leave the rest as it pertains to your own writing practice, it's often tempting to internalize teachings wholesale. Especially when you're getting started and feel you don't yet know what you don't know.

As someone who has put hundreds of thousands of hours and words of craft and industry guidance into the writing reference world across my platforms, podcasts, articles, and books, I'm guilty of contributing tons of "you should" and "never do this" to the conversation. But I hope you'll examine *these* ideas to see if they work for you, too.

This is your permission to interpret "show, don't tell" and all the other well-meaning pieces of writing and publishing advice you hear or read in your own way. To do what makes sense for you. To fight for not only the "what" you want to do, but also the "how."

I hope I've managed to both show *and* tell you a new mode of thinking about the writing craft. And if not? You have my permission—not that you need it—to forge your own path toward a good story anyway.

RESOURCES FOR WRITERS

I've spent almost two decades creating educational materials for writers and designing courses, books, and services focused on craft and industry topics. Please check out my resources and offerings.

Webinars

I regularly teach free webinars about query letters, character, interiority, plot, and first pages. Some webinars offer the opportunity for live feedback. Find a current list of my upcoming presentations and workshops here:

https://goodstorycompany.com/workshops

I can also Zoom in to your critique group or design a bespoke talk for a writing retreat or conference on any number of industry and craft subjects.

Editorial Services, Ghostwriting, and Writing Workshops

If you enjoyed this book, consider getting personalized one-on-one feedback from me. My specialty is deep developmental editing with a character focus. Alternatively, I'm happy to step in as a discreet ghostwriter or offer direct ghost revision to execute changes directly. We can also work together in a small group writing workshop intensive setting.

Developmental Editing Services:

https://marykole.com

Ghost Revision and Ghostwriting Services:

https://manuscriptstudio.com

Story Mastermind Small Group Writing Workshops:

https://storymastermind.com

Free Story Mastermind Outline Framework:

https://bit.ly/novel-outline

Courses

It is my (perhaps manic) goal to create as many writing resources in as many formats as possible. I hope you find the below courses useful. I'm always grateful when a written or recorded version of me can be of service.

Writing Mastery Academy Character Class:

With Jessica Brody, of *Save the Cat Writes a Novel* fame!

https://www.writingmastery.com

Writing Blueprints Submission Resource:

If a deep dive into the submission process sounds helpful, this self-paced course contains over ten hours of instruction. You'll get access to agent interviews, over thirty handouts, and a comprehensive step-by-step submission guide.

https://bit.ly/kolesub

LinkedIn Learning:

My popular Crafting Dynamic Characters class is also available on this platform.

https://www.linkedin.com/learning/crafting-dynamic-characters/

Udemy:

These budget-friendly classes cover assorted writing and publishing topics in an easy-to-digest format.

https://www.udemy.com/user/mary-kole/

Good Story Company

In 2019, I founded Good Story Company as an umbrella brand so my amazing team and I could collaborate in the service of writing and writers. GSC is where you'll find our most comprehensive library of resources and services. You can also sign up for our email newsletter and follow us on social media to get our most current updates.

Good Story Company:

https://goodstorycompany.com

Good Story Podcast:

https://goodstorypodcast.com

Good Story YouTube Channel:

https://youtube.com/goodstory

Thriving Writers Membership:

https://goodstorycompany.com/membership

Good Story Marketing:

https://goodstorycompany.com/marketing

Workshops and Events:

https://goodstorycompany.com/workshops

Thriving Writers Substack:

https://goodstoryco.substack.com/

ACKNOWLEDGMENTS

Damn. This one took some guts. First, to *identify* my problem with "show, don't tell" over many many many *many* years of working with stories and teaching writing and writers. Second, to consider why this maxim is so limiting and misleading. Third, to collect examples of effective telling and study why they work. And fourth, to tie it all together in a way that—I sure hope—makes sense to a third party *outside* the frenzied motorcycle cage of my own brain.

There's also the inherent tension of teaching writing rules, guidelines, and best practices for fifteen years, then turning around and slaughtering the editorial industry's most sacred cow. (🐮 Moo.) Oh, well. YOLO.

As always, my team at Good Story Company allows me to do the work I love. Thank you Kristen Overman, Amy Wilson, Rhiannon Richardson, and Kaylee Pereyra. Thank you also to the editorial clients who've trusted me over the years.

Love, love, love to John Cusick, Julie Murphy, my Westie Besties (Lauren Burris and Scott Marasigan), Todd, Theo, Finn, Ella, Gertie, Olive, and Luna.

WAIT! BEFORE YOU GO!

If you enjoyed this book, there are **three small things** you can do to make a big difference to me and Good Story Company. Thank you so much for your time, kind attention, and consideration!

Subscribe to Our Newsletter

Our respectful, short, and non-spammy newsletter features all of our latest and greatest free resources, workshops, events, and critique opportunities. Go here to sign up:

https://bit.ly/hellogsc

Leave an Honest Review

Please also consider leaving a review for this title with your retailer of choice, as well as Goodreads. I love getting feedback of my own, and testimonials help our discoverability and marketing efforts, allowing us to reach more writers.

Reach Out

Finally, I'd love to hear your experience and celebrate your accomplishments. If you run into trouble in the writing and publishing worlds, don't be a stranger, either. Drop me a line:

mary@goodstorycompany.com

ALSO BY MARY KOLE

Writing Irresistible Kidlit: The Ultimate Guide to Crafting Fiction for Young Adult and Middle Grade Readers

———

Writing Irresistible Picture Books: Insider Insights Into Crafting Compelling Modern Stories for Young Readers

Writing Irresistible Picture Books Workbook

———

Irresistible Query Letters: 40+ Real World Query Letters with Literary Agent Feedback

Irresistible Query Letters Workbook

———

How to Write a Book Now: Craft Concepts, Mindset Shifts, and Encouragement to Inspire Your Creative Writing

———

Writing Interiority: Crafting Irresistible Characters

Writing Interiority Workbook

———

Writing Irresistible First Pages: How to Craft Compelling Story Openings That Will Hook Gatekeepers and Readers

Writing Irresistible First Pages Workbook

———

Show and Tell: Going Beyond Creative Writing's Most Enduring Paradigm

NOTES

AI Transparency Statement

i. Brewin, Kester. "Why I wrote an AI transparency statement for my book, and think other authors should too." *The Guardian*, April 4, 2024. https://www.theguardian.com/books/2024/apr/04/why-i-wrote-an-ai-transparency-statement-for-my-book-and-think-other-authors-should-too.

1. The Wisdom and Pitfalls of "Show, Don't Tell"

i. Jesse Q. Sutanto, *Vera Wong's Unsolicited Advice for Murderers* (New York: Berkley, 2023), 17.

2. Understanding Telling

i. Ann Napolitano, *Hello Beautiful* (New York: The Dial Press, 2022), 5.
ii. Ibid, 26-27.
iii. Alix E. Harrow, *Starling House* (New York: Tor, 2023), 3.
iv. Sally Rooney, *Beautiful World, Where Are You* (New York: Farrar, Straus, and Giroux, 2021), 61.
v. Riley Sager, *The House Across the Lake* (New York: Dutton, 2022), 110.
vi. Jenny Hollander, *Everyone Who Can Forgive Me Is Dead* (New York: Minotaur, 2024), 259.
vii. Angie Kim, *Happiness Falls* (London: Hogarth, 2023), 115.
viii. Byron Graves, *Rez Ball* (New York: Heartdrum, 2023), 53.
ix. Ibid, 53.
x. Hanya Yanagihara, *A Little Life* (New York: Knopf Doubleday, 2015), 41.
xi. Venita Blackburn, *Dead in Long Beach, California* (New York: MCD Books, 2024), 9.
xii. Rory Power, *Wilder Girls* (New York: Delacorte Press, 2019), 25.

3. Showing and Telling Character

i. Kelly Barnhill, *When Women Were Dragons* (New York: Knopf Doubleday, 2022), 124.

4. Sense of Self, Objective, and Motivation

i. Claire Pooley, *How to Age Disgracefully* (New York: Penguin Books, 2024), 47.

ii. Krystal Sutherland, *The Invocations* (New York: Nancy Paulsen Books, 2024), 372.

iii. Ashley Winstead, *Midnight Is the Darkest Hour* (Naperville: Sourcebooks Landmark, 2023), 8.

iv. Kaveh Akbar, *Martyr!* (New York: Alfred A. Knopf, 2024), 290.

v. Alison Espach, *The Wedding People* (New York: Henry Holt, 2024), 58.

vi. Coco Mellors, *Blue Sisters* (New York: Ballantine Books, 2024), 246-247.

vii. Hernan Diaz, *Trust* (New York: Riverhead Books, 2022), 57.

viii. Ada Calhoun, *Crush* (New York: Viking, 2025), 16.

ix. Gabrielle Zevin, *Tomorrow, and Tomorrow, and Tomorrow* (New York: Alfred A. Knopf, 2023), 35.

x. Alix E. Harrow, *Starling House* (New York: Tor, 2023), 239.

xi. Emma Cook, *You Can't Hurt Me* (London: Orion Publishing Group, 2024), 43.

xii. Juhea Kim, *City of Night Birds* (New York: Ecco, 2024), 62.

xiii. Coco Mellors, *Blue Sisters* (New York: Ballantine Books, 2024), 5.

xiv. Alison Espach, *The Wedding People* (New York: Henry Holt, 2024), 334.

xv. Kelly Barnhill, *When Women Were Dragons* (New York: Knopf Doubleday, 2022), 159-160.

5. Backstory and Worldview

i. Emma Cline, *The Guest* (New York: Random House, 2022), 8.

ii. Claire Pooley, *How to Age Disgracefully* (New York: Penguin Books, 2024), 165.

iii. Marcus Kliewer, *We Used to Live Here* (New York: Emily Bestler Books, 2024), 55.

iv. Yangsze Choo, *The Fox Wife* (New York: Henry Holt, 2024), 13.

v. Jenny Hollander, *Everyone Who Can Forgive Me Is Dead* (New York: Minotaur, 2024), 25.

vi. Jeneva Rose, *Home Is Where the Bodies Are* (Ashland: Blackstone Publishing, 2024), 67.

vii. Jami Attenberg, *A Reason to See You Again* (New York: Ecco, 2024), 2-3.

viii. Hernan Diaz, *Trust* (New York: Riverhead Books, 2022), 30-31.

ix. Catherine Steadman, *Look in the Mirror* (New York: Ballantine Books, 2024), 83.

x. Sarah Harman, *All the Other Mothers Hate Me* (New York: G.P. Putnam's Sons, 2025), 179.

xi. Angie Kim, *Happiness Falls* (London: Hogarth, 2023), 8.

xii. Clémence Michallon, *The Quiet Tenant* (New York: Alfred A. Knopf, 2023), 33.

xiii. Marcus Kliewer, *We Used to Live Here* (New York: Emily Bestler Books, 2024), 209.

xiv. Emma Noyes, *Guy's Girl* (New York: Berkley, 2023), 21.

xv. Nicola Solvinic, *The Hunter's Daughter* (New York: Berkley, 2024), 11.

xvi. Raven Leilani, *Luster* (New York: Farrar, Straus, and Giroux, 2020), 192.

xvii. Coco Mellors, *Blue Sisters* (New York: Ballantine Books, 2024), 93.

xviii. V.E. Schwab, *Bury Our Bones in the Midnight Soil* (New York: Tor, 2025), 15.

6. Wound, Need, and Inner Struggle

i. Fran Littlewood, *Amazing Grace Adams* (New York: Henry Holt, 2023), 79.

ii. Alison Espach, *The Wedding People* (New York: Henry Holt, 2024), 171.

iii. Ibid, 363.

iv. Del Sandeen, *This Cursed House* (New York: Berkley, 2024), 84-85.

v. R.F. Kuang, *Yellowface* (New York: William Morrow, 2023), 258.

vi. Claire Lombardo, *Same As It Ever Was* (New York: Knopf Doubleday, 2024), 256.

vii. Kelly Barnhill, *When Women Were Dragons* (New York: Knopf Doubleday, 2022), 203.

viii. Betsy Lerner, *Shred Sisters* (New York: Grove Press, 2024), 73.

ix. Elisa Albert, *Human Blues* (New York: Avid Reader Press, 2023), 1-2.

x. Dan Gemeinhart, *The Remarkable Journey of Coyote Sunrise* (New York: Henry Holt & Company Books for Young Readers, 2019), 123.

7. Secondary Characters and Relationships

i. Emma Noyes, *Guy's Girl* (New York: Berkley, 2023), 8.

ii. Alison Espach, *The Wedding People* (New York: Henry Holt, 2024), 231.

iii. Ibid, 255-256.

iv. Ashley Winstead, *Midnight Is the Darkest Hour* (Naperville: Sourcebooks Landmark, 2023), 32.

v. Kelly Barnhill, *When Women Were Dragons* (New York: Knopf Doubleday, 2022), 28.

vi. Tess Gunty, *The Rabbit Hutch* (New York: Alfred A. Knopf, 2022), 52.

vii. Betsy Lerner, *Shred Sisters* (New York: Grove Press, 2024), 19.

viii. Claire Lombardo, *Same As It Ever Was* (New York: Knopf Doubleday, 2024), 99-100.

ix. Jessica Knoll, *Bright Young Women* (New York: Marysue Rucci Books, 2023), 61.

x. Ibid, 140.

xi. Coco Mellors, *Blue Sisters* (New York: Ballantine Books, 2024), 176.

8. Plot, Conflict, and Stakes

i. Sarai Johnson, *Grown Women* (New York: Harper, 2024), 75.

ii. Kay Chronister, *The Bog Wife* (Berkeley: Counterpoint Press, 2024), 95.

iii. Andrea Bartz, *We Were Never Here* (New York: Ballantine Books, 2021), 59.

iv. Catherine Steadman, *Look in the Mirror* (New York: Ballantine Books, 2024), 161.

v. Sarah Harman, *All the Other Mothers Hate Me* (New York: G.P. Putnam's Sons, 2025), 345.

vi. Nicola Solvinic, *The Hunter's Daughter* (New York: Berkley, 2024), 178-179.

vii. Naomi Alderman, *The Future* (New York: Simon & Schuster, 2023), 14.

viii. Jesse Q. Sutanto, *Vera Wong's Unsolicited Advice for Murderers* (New York: Berkley, 2023), 167-168.

ix. Joelle Wellington, *The Blonde Dies First* (New York: Simon & Schuster Books for Young Readers, 2024), 179.

10. Telling About Setting and World

i. Byron Graves, *Rez Ball* (New York: Heartdrum, 2023), 27.

ii. Riley Sager, *The House Across the Lake* (New York: Dutton, 2022), 36.

iii. Gabrielle Zevin, *Tomorrow, and Tomorrow, and Tomorrow* (New York: Alfred A. Knopf, 2023), 27.

iv. R.F. Kuang, *Yellowface* (New York: William Morrow, 2023), 6.

v. Miranda July, *All Fours* (New York: Riverhead Books, 2024), 15-16.

vi. Randy Ribay, *Everything We Never Had* (New York: Kokila Books, 2024), 14-15.

vii. Percival Everett, *James* (New York: Knopf Doubleday, 2024), 27.

viii. Isabel Ibañez, *What the River Knows* (New York: Wednesday Books, 2023), 4-5.

ix. Sabaa Tahir, *Heir* (New York: G.P. Puntam's Sons Books for Young Readers, 2024), 86.

x. V.E. Schwab, *Bury Our Bones in the Midnight Soil* (New York: Tor, 2025), 159.

xi. Krystal Sutherland, *The Invocations* (New York: Nancy Paulsen Books, 2024), 5.

xii. Yangsze Choo, *The Fox Wife* (New York: Henry Holt, 2024), 64.

xiii. Ibid, 224.

xiv. Rebecca Yarros, *The Fourth Wing* (Fort Collins: Red Tower Books, 2023), 10.

www.ingramcontent.com/pod-product-compliance
Lightning Source LLC
Chambersburg PA
CBHW070105030426
42335CB00016B/2014